# I GOT MY

# DREAM

# JOB

### *and So Can You*

## 7 Steps to Creating Your
## Ideal Career After College

# PETE LEIBMAN

**AMACOM**

AMERICAN MANAGEMENT ASSOCIATION
New York · Atlanta · Brussels · Chicago · Mexico City · San Francisco
Shanghai · Tokyo · Toronto · Washington, D.C.

Bulk discounts available. For details visit:
www.amacombooks.org/go/specialsales
Or contact special sales:
Phone: 800-250-5308
Email: specialsls@amanet.org
View all the AMACOM titles at: www.amacombooks.org

LIBRARY OF CONGRESS CATALOGING-IN-PUBLICATION DATA
Leibman, Pete, 1981–
    I got my dream job and so can you : 7 steps to creating your ideal career after college / Pete Leibman.
        p. cm.
    Includes bibliographical references and index.
    ISBN-13: 978-0-8144-2020-1 (pbk.)
    ISBN-10: 0-8144-2020-6 (pbk.)
  1. Job hunting. 2. Vocational guidance. I. Title.
    HF5382.7.L45 2012
    650.14—dc23
                                        2011033266

**About AMA**

American Management Association (www.amanet.org) is a world leader in talent development, advancing the skills of individuals to drive business success. Our mission is to support the goals of individuals and organizations through a complete range of products and services, including classroom and virtual seminars, webcasts, webinars, podcasts, conferences, corporate and government solutions, business books, and research. AMA's approach to improving performance combines experiential learning—learning through doing—with opportunities for ongoing professional growth at every step of one's career journey.

.
Printing number

10 9 8 7 6 5 4 3

# CONTENTS

# PART II

## Skyrocket Your Career with Step #7

## (B.E.P.R.O.)

# ACKNOWLEDGMENTS

First and foremost, this book is dedicated to my mom, my dad, and my brother Matt. Thank you for always supporting my dreams. Words could never express how much I love you and appreciate you.

Thank you to those who shared their stories in this book and to all my friends and colleagues who shared their ideas for the book (including Allie Miller, Asha Tyson, Bithiah LaFontant, Brian Elderbroom, Brian Lee, Calvin Scott, Chrissy Mack, Darrell Bennett, Greg Turner, Jay Kreider, Jeremy Zelman, Jon Foster, Kim Foley, Laura Neesen, Marshall Brown, Matt Dershewitz, Nick Macri, Nishant Tulsian, Paayal Malhotra, Pai Dayanzadeh, Rachna Sethi, Ron Culberson, Stu Miller, and Wolf Rinke).

Thank you to Leslie Kendrick, Howe Burch, and David Cope and to the incredible staff with the Washington Wizards (especially Susan O'Malley, Mark Schiponi, Jerry Murphy, Jim Anderson, and Bill Anderson).

Thank you to Tom Chillot, Mike Murray, and the wonderful staff at TMA.

Thank you to Anne Loehr and Grace Freedson, and to the phenomenal staff at AMACOM (especially Ellen Kadin, Erika Spelman, and William Helms).

Thank you to the brilliant authors and speakers who initially inspired me from afar to pursue a similar career path (especially Anthony Robbins, Brendon Burchard, Brian Tracy, Darren Hardy, Denis Waitley, Jack Canfield, Joel Osteen, Sam Horn, and Stephen Covey).

I am forever grateful for all the wonderful people who have supported me throughout my life. It's impossible to thank everyone who has influenced me, so I apologize to those I missed. Thank you all for helping to make my dreams come true. . . .

# INTRODUCTION

*My Story and Why You Should Read This Book*

> "Never measure the height of a mountain until you have reached the top. Then you will see how low it was."
>
> —DAG HAMMARSKJOLD, UNITED NATIONS SECRETARY-GENERAL AND
>
> NOBEL PEACE PRIZE WINNER

January 31, 1989: at Madison Square Garden (six minutes before tip-off for Knicks vs. Pacers)

A ball bounced over to us, so I grabbed it and looked up. My father and I were standing right next to the scorer's table at MSG. There were no security concerns at that time about fans being next to the court.

Chuck Person, a player on the Pacers, ran over to me and put his hands up. He looked like he was 12 feet tall.

I gave him the best chest-pass of my life. He caught the ball and said, "Hey, little man, thanks for grabbing that. What's your name?"

I smiled, and in my high-pitched, meek, seven-year-old voice said, "My name's Pete."

Chuck smiled back and said, "Well, Pete, this one's for you." Then he turned around and launched a shot from where he was standing, 25 feet from the basket. It zipped through the net. *Swoosh!*

He turned his head back to me, smiled, winked, and ran over to his team's bench.

That was the first time I said to myself that I was going to make it to the NBA when I grew up.

## April 8, 2003: at Johns Hopkins University (in my dorm room)

I was freaking out. How had I gotten into this position?

I had done everything that you are supposed to do as a student to prepare for your career, but it had gotten me nowhere. In one month, I was going to be graduating from college, and I had no idea where I was going to live or work. Not exactly the reward I expected after busting my butt for four years.

Ever since I had been a little kid, basketball had been my obsession. When I got to college at Johns Hopkins University and learned that I could combine my love of basketball with my passion for business, I knew exactly what my dream job would be: a marketing and sales position with an NBA franchise.

Unfortunately, it looked like that dream would never become a reality.

I had spent four years maintaining a high GPA, paying my dues in internships, and scraping by with part-time jobs that barely paid minimum wage. I also spent my entire senior year applying to advertised jobs, participating in on-campus recruiting, and attending career fairs all over Baltimore and Washington, D.C. However, I still had no leads on a job with an NBA team or with any organization connected to sports.

I had come close the summer before my senior year, when I landed an interview for an internship position with the NBA's Washington Wizards. However, the Wizards had rejected me and selected another candidate, one who I assumed was more qualified and credentialed.

Now the pressure was starting to mount, and I was really getting tired of friends and family asking what I was going to do after college. I didn't know the answer.

As I checked my email that afternoon, I noticed that the Baltimore chapter of the American Marketing Association was going to have a career workshop for local students in four days, on Saturday, April 12, 2003. I also noticed that one of the featured speakers was going to be a man named Howe Burch. At the time, Howe was a senior executive for Fila, the sports marketing company.

A light bulb went off in my head as I thought to myself: *"Well, he works in sports. Nothing else has worked for me, so why don't I go to the event and ask him for some advice. What do I have to lose?"*

Little did I know that simple decision would change my life *forever*.

Six weeks later, I found myself in a private interview with Susan O'Malley, the team president for the Washington Wizards at the time. (In Chapter 6, I'll fill in the blanks on how I got the interview.) The following week, the Wizards offered me a full-time position in their front office, even though I was only 21 years old and had no industry experience. I didn't want to appear too eager when they made their offer, so I waited three seconds before accepting the job.

Over the next five years, the Washington Wizards actually paid me (very well, in fact) to brainstorm and execute strategies that would increase attendance at their home games. I also got to:

- Watch games from courtside (a slight upgrade from my usual seat locations as a fan in college).

- Fly on an NBA team plane (a slight upgrade from my usual modes of transportation as a student in college).

- Mingle with political leaders, TV personalities, and multimillionaire CEOs. (It is absurd how much money these people spend.)

- Dunk on an NBA court before a game. (Some white guys *can* jump, thank you very much.)

- Shake hands with an ex-NBA player who was 7'7" tall. (His fingers were like bananas.)

- Scrimmage against WNBA All-Stars, including Chamique

Holdsclaw and Alana Beard. (I'm still trying to catch my breath six years later.)

► Attend an NBA All-Star Game after-party with the players. (I have never felt so short in my life.)

► Have my own private office inside the Verizon Center in Washington, D.C. (Well, I started in a cubicle the size of a closet, but I got my own office eventually!)

While the perks were great, they were not the best part of my position. More important, my job gave me a platform to create programs that made dreams come true for other sports fans, and my job enabled me to fulfill *my* lifelong dream to make it to the NBA (even though I didn't make it as a player).

I got my dream job and so can you!

• • •

This book will teach you *everything* you need to know to get your dream job and create your ideal career as a young professional. While this book features a number of sports analogies and stories from my life, this book is the blueprint for getting any job you want *in any industry*.

## WHY YOU NEED THIS BOOK

Most people will spend about 5 million minutes at work throughout their lives. Yes, 5 million minutes! (Do the math: 60 minutes in an hour, 40 hours a week, 50 weeks out of the year, and 40 years at work.)

Given how much of your life will be spent at work, isn't it worth it to spend some time to identify and pursue your dream job? It's going to be pretty hard to feel happy and fulfilled if half of your waking minutes after college are spent working in a job you hate.

It's so easy to take for granted the importance of being proactive with your career, especially if you are a student who has never worked a full-time job before. A 2010 Conference Board survey featured on www.USAToday.com showed that job dissatisfaction was at an all-time high, with workers under the age of 25 being the unhappiest of all.

So, why does this happen?

Well, people don't end up in dead-end jobs because of a lack of talent or because of the economy. Instead, most people just aim way too low. Most people settle for the first job they can get, while deluding themselves into believing that they will go after their dreams later in life.

There are millions of students and young professionals out there today who are depressed or angry about the direction (or lack of direction) of their careers. You are definitely not alone if you feel that way as well. You may feel lost because you do not know what you want to do. You may feel defeated because others have brainwashed you into believing that your dream is not possible to achieve. You may feel frustrated because nothing seems to be working for you.

I have been there.

When it comes to my career, I have felt lost, defeated, and frustrated on more than one occasion. However, certain beliefs and actions have helped me get my dream job twice while I was in my 20s (first as an NBA executive and now as an entrepreneur, speaker, career coach, and published author).

I'm certainly not the first person to write a book on getting your dream job after college, and I will not be the last. However, this book is well worth your time for three main reasons:

1. *I am part of your generation, so I understand your situation.* Most career books written for students and young professionals are written by authors from a totally different generation. Despite their wisdom and positive intentions, they grew up in a totally different world from the one you and I grew up in, and most of them have a very different perspective about your job search.

2.   *This book is based on real-world results.* Networking, marketing yourself, interviewing, identifying your passions and talents . . . none of these processes came easily to me. I struggled before I succeeded. I was not blessed with some inborn ability to conduct a job search or to achieve my dreams. I had to figure everything out on my own through trial-and-error because it was all so unclear to me. I wrote this book to teach you how to get your dream job faster and with less effort than you might imagine is possible. The strategies in this book are not concepts I am simply passing along from a textbook I studied, a survey I read on www.monster.com, or a seminar I attended. Everything in this book is based on my firsthand, real-world experience. This book also features success stories of 10 other young professionals who recently landed their dream jobs (both with organizations you might not know of and with well-known employers including Microsoft, the U.S. State Department, and Teach For America). Who wants to read another boring, ineffective textbook?

3.   *This book is a comprehensive, step-by-step blueprint.* I assumed you would not want to check out 27 other job search books after reading this one. This book was written in such a way that you would not have to read one more book on this topic. Got a question about résumés? The answer is in here. Got a question about interviewing? The answer is in here. Got a question about networking? The answer is in here. Got a question about LinkedIn? The answer is in here. Not sure what you want to do? Well, the answer is *in you*, but this book will help you identify the answer. You get the point. . . .

By the time you are finished with this book, you will know 10 times as much as I knew about success and happiness when I started my journey from college to career. I have taken thousands of hours of private study, real-world application, and self-reflection and synthesized the greatest lessons into a highly organized framework that you can easily follow to take charge of your career *now*.

## GETTING YOUR DREAM JOB IS S.I.M.P.L.E.

Most people completely misunderstand the point of work and life. It's not to "plug along" in some job that you hate just so you can pay your bills. The point of life is to go after your dreams with everything you have! To get your dream job, you just need to follow my six steps that spell out S.I.M.P.L.E.—*Start*, *Identify*, *Makeover*, *Plan*, *Look*, and *Execute*—which make up Part I of this book. (After you get your dream job, Step 7, discussed later, will help you create your ideal career.)

If you don't have your dream job yet, there are only six possible reasons why:

1. *You haven't started the process.* Chapter 1 (Most Career Advice Is Wrong) and Chapter 2 (*Start*) will revolutionize the way you look at a job search and help you begin your journey for your dream job.

2. *You lack focus and commitment.* Chapter 3 (*Identify*) will help you think big and determine what *your* dream job is.

3. *You don't know how to present yourself or you are not aware of how you are presenting yourself.* Chapter 4 (*Makeover*) will show you how you can look like a million bucks in person, on paper, and online.

4. *You have no strategy or a poor strategy.* Chapter 5 (*Plan*) will help you design a bulletproof plan for getting hired in any industry as quickly as possible.

5. *You are not looking for jobs the right way.* Chapter 6 (*Look*) will teach you the four best ways to look for jobs so that you can get hired with less effort than you might think is possible.

6. *You don't know how to seal the deal.* Chapter 7 (*Execute*) will show you how to ace any interview process.

## SKYROCKET YOUR CAREER (B.E.P.R.O.)

Getting your dream job is not the final destination, however. Part II of the book teaches you Step #7 ("Be Professional") on how to create your ideal career after college. To be professional, you need to understand my five secrets for career success that spell out B.E.P.R.O.—*Belief, Excellence, Performance, Relationships,* and Out-of-Office Life—which make up Part II of this book.

The goal should not be to get your dream job and just try to "keep it." It drives me crazy when authors write books about "keeping" your job. Come on, people. Are we really setting the bar so low that we are just trying *to not get fired*?! Your goal should be to reach your full potential and be your best. That's what Part II will help you do.

► Chapter 8 (*Belief*) will show you how to develop a winning mindset for your career.

► Chapter 9 (*Excellence*) will show you how to develop an impeccable reputation.

► Chapter 10 (*Performance*) will show you how to deliver groundbreaking, innovative results for your employer.

► Chapter 11 (*Relationships*) will show you how to build rock-solid professional relationships in and out of your organization.

► Chapter 12 (Out-of-Office Life) will show you how to take charge of your life outside work, so that you can be even better at work.

I've also included a bonus chapter if you have any entrepreneurial aspirations. Chapter 13 (Be an Entrepreneur) will show you what to do if you dream of running your own business someday.

## NOW IS THE BEST TIME EVER TO GET YOUR DREAM JOB—SERIOUSLY

You might not believe me yet, but this book will show you why *this is the best time ever to get your dream job and skyrocket your career*, no matter what you want to do. When I was a student in college, there was no comprehensive, step-by-step framework on how to break into and rise quickly in any organization. I had to figure it out on my own through trial-and-error, and that is good news for you.

This book will not bombard you with hundreds of random tips that leave you feeling overwhelmed and directionless. Instead, this book features a systematic, proven process that you can easily follow to create the career of your dreams. In addition, when I was in college, social media barely existed, and that made my job search much more cumbersome than yours has to be. Thanks to the Internet, it is now easier than ever before to brand yourself as a high-value job-seeker and to get connected with influential people who are in a position to hire you. This book will also show you a number of creative, little-known secrets for advancing your career through the power of innovative online tools like LinkedIn.

Even though I got my dream job twice in my 20s, I definitely struggled along the way. I wrote this book because I want your journey to be easier than mine was. I believe to the bottom of my soul that you can break into (and rise quickly in) any organization, any industry, any economy, if you apply the strategies discussed in this book.

Are you ready to get your dream job and skyrocket your career?! Then, let's get started. . . .

• • •

**BONUS:** Visit www.BestCareerBook.com for a FREE welcome video and for FREE job-search bonuses not included in this book.

# PART I

# GETTING YOUR DREAM JOB IS S.I.M.P.L.E.

# CHAPTER 1

# MOST CAREER ADVICE IS WRONG

> "The trouble with advice is that you can't tell if it's good or bad until you've taken it."
>
> —FRANK TYGER, EDITORIAL CARTOONIST AND COLUMNIST

## WHO HAVE YOU BEEN LISTENING TO?

Everyone loves giving career advice to students and young professionals. Everyone thinks he is a career expert. You want to know the truth?

*Very few people know what they are talking about.*

When I reflect back on the career advice given to me over the last 10 years, I realize that most of it was inaccurate, and some of it actually stunted my development. Here is the secret: You have to be very coachable, open-minded, and willing to ask for advice, while at the same time skeptical about what you believe to be true.

Always consider the source. Funnel all advice through your own filter. Does the person's viewpoint sound logical? What is the perspective of the person giving you advice? Is this someone you should be listening to? Has this person gotten her dream job? Does she love her work? Do you want to be like her?

In case it's not clear, I am not saying that I am the only person worth listening to or that I am always right. Nope—I want you to challenge everything I tell you as well, so that you can make decisions on your own.

Here are 10 little-known job search and career success secrets I wish someone had told me when I was a student.

## 1. Employers Are Nervous, Too

You are not the only one who is anxious about the hiring process. The people doing the hiring are nervous, too. A bad hire can cost an organization thousands of dollars. Employers are even more nervous when times are tough. I didn't fully understand this mindset until I started my own business in 2009 and considered hiring my first employee. No matter what organization you want to work for and no matter what type of work you want to do, you will find that every employer and hiring person has six primary concerns about job candidates and new hires. One of your goals as a jobseeker is to make sure employers have no reason to believe that you have any of the following six traits:

- *Dishonest.* If an employer doesn't think you can be trusted, you aren't getting hired.

- *Lazy.* If an employer thinks you will not work hard or you will need your hand held at all times, you aren't getting hired.

- *Difficult.* If an employer thinks you are going to be a pain in the neck to manage or work with, you aren't getting hired.

- *Uncommitted.* If an employer thinks you might bolt for another job one month into your employment, you aren't getting hired.

- *Unprofessional.* If an employer thinks you might be a source of embarrassment (in person or online), you aren't getting hired. With the explosion of social media, this is becoming more of a concern.

▶ *Unqualified.* If an employer doesn't think you can get the job done better than anyone else, you aren't getting hired. Note: If you satisfy the first five fears, this last concern can often be eliminated. As a senior executive from a Fortune 500 company told me in 2011, "We hire for attitude and train for skill."

## 2. Every Employer Has the Same Four Needs

It's really easy to figure out what employers want. No matter what your dream job might be, *every* employer needs four variables from potential employees. Your task as a job-seeker is to prove that you can deliver these four needs better than anyone else:

▶ *Belief.* Employers want people who believe in themselves, and they want people who believe in the mission of their organization. One of the questions you will be asked (directly or indirectly) in any interview is "Why do you want this job?" If you don't have a great answer to that question, that's a sign you should be looking elsewhere. You aren't doing yourself or anyone else a favor by pursuing jobs you aren't really excited about, and you aren't doing yourself a favor by being overly humble.

▶ *Excellence.* It doesn't matter what your GPA is or how talented you are if your integrity is questionable or if you look like a slob. Excellence is essential for getting hired and for achieving career success. If you are still a student, you will be amazed after college at how easy it is to stand out in a good way at work. Most employees just do the bare minimum or worse. A little extra effort multiplies quickly over time, and it is always noticed by the people at the top.

▶ *People/Communication skills.* Regardless of your employer, you will have a boss, you will have colleagues, and your organization will serve other people, whether they are clients, customers, patients, donors, voters, subscribers, or students. To achieve career success, you must get along well with other people, and you must be able to communicate clearly and effectively with them.

► *Results.* The desired results are different based on the employer and your job, but employers hire people for one reason: to solve problems. Period. When you demonstrate that you deliver top-notch results, you will almost always get hired faster and promoted faster.

## 3. The Best Way to Get Your Dream Job Is to Stop Looking for Jobs and Look for People

Employers don't want to hire people they think are dishonest, lazy, difficult, uncommitted, unprofessional, or unqualified. They do want to hire people who have belief, excellence, people/communication skills, and the ability to deliver results. This presents a challenge, doesn't it? How can you possibly show an employer you are the right type of person if you are relying on your résumé alone to sell yourself?

The answer? You can't.

As a student in college, I was the right type of person, my résumé was perfect, and I spent hundreds of hours applying for jobs the traditional way. Do you know where it had me headed? My parents' basement!

When I finally ignored my networking fears and looked for people, I actually landed my dream job very easily. When you find the right people and impress those people, everything else will take care of itself. The U.S. Bureau of Labor Statistics estimates that more than 70 percent of jobs are filled through networking and personal contacts. Getting a job is a true "relationship sale." It is literally one person or a group of people "buying" another person. As a result, doesn't it make sense to rely on other people to get hired?

Because most jobs are filled behind the scenes through personal contacts and networking, most jobs are also never advertised. If you rely only on advertised jobs during your job search, you will be missing somewhere between 50 and 80 percent of the opportunities that are actually out there. The only way to find those jobs and crack the "hidden job market" is to talk to people working in the organizations and industry you want to hire you.

Don't worry if you think you don't know anyone or if the word "networking" confuses or intimidates you. I didn't think I knew anyone when I was starting my career, and networking did not come naturally to me either. Chapters 5 and 6 will teach you everything you need to know on the subject.

## 4. Employers Look for Reasons to Exclude You, Not Include You

During a job search, your appearance and your behavior are put under a microscope, as employers make very quick assumptions about you based on your job search habits and communication skills. This is one reason why first impressions are so imperative to your success. Submit a résumé with one typo, and employers will assume you don't take pride in your work. Be rude to a secretary when you schedule an interview, and employers will assume you will also be rude to your colleagues or customers. Show up 10 minutes late for an interview, and employers will assume you won't be reliable on the job either. This might sound harsh, but it's all employers have to evaluate you. You get only one chance to make a first impression during your job search.

The good news is that this works the other way as well. Ask thought-provoking questions during an interview, and employers will assume you are smart and enthusiastic. Send a well-written thank-you note after an interview, and they will assume you will be thorough and pleasant on the job. Give a firm handshake, and they will assume you are confident and trustworthy.

You must put your best foot forward at all times throughout your entire job search. Employers make fast, sometimes inaccurate, judgments about your character, personality, and intelligence based on behaviors that may seem minor to you.

## 5. Every Great Employer Is *Always* Hiring

I actually left my dream job in the NBA in 2008, which I'll discuss later in this chapter. When I conducted a search then for a full-time job, I was able to get offers from three different organizations for jobs that each would have paid me at least $100,000 to $125,000 in year one. This was at the start of the recession when I was only 26 years old. While none of the employers was *officially* hiring, each organization was willing to *create* a job for me because of how I approached them. Two of the organizations were also in industries I had no experience in at all.

Every employer can and should create a job any time the right person comes along. Hiring someone is nothing more than an investment. If you can prove to the hiring decision maker that you will provide a positive Return on Investment (i.e., your value will significantly exceed your salary), then it would be stupid for the employer *not* to hire you. Great employers recognize this. Employers that don't understand this are organizations you shouldn't want to work for anyway.

If an organization is not consistently looking to hire top talent, then that organization is headed absolutely nowhere in the future. Great organizations recognize that they need to have a pipeline full of talent since they will inevitably experience change and turnover.

If someone tells you his organization is not hiring, he either doesn't want to hire *you* or he isn't the real decision maker.

## 6. Your Job Search Strategy Impacts the Interview Process and How You Will Be Treated After Being Hired

No employer will admit this publicly because every employer wants everyone to think its hiring and HR practices are uniform for all applicants and employees. Based on my own experience and some off-the-record conversations with employers, that's a load of garbage.

Without exception, interviews I have managed to land through job boards or traditional channels have always been *much* tougher than interviews I have gotten through personal contacts and networking. This makes sense. If employers don't know you or the person who referred you, they should test you more during the interview process.

When I walked into the Wizards' offices back in 2003 to interview for a full-time job, I was not "some kid found through Monster.com." Instead, I was "the kid referred by their former senior executive."

What do you think that did for my credibility before I even showed up for the interview? My first impression was taken care of well before I ever walked into their offices. Perhaps more important, what do you think it did for my confidence? I walked in with a halo around my head, and after I got over my initial anxiety about interviewing with the team president, I felt much more relaxed than in interviews with other companies where I lacked a personal connection. (Of course, you still need to prepare impeccably for every interview.)

The way you come into contact with an employer also dictates your ability to negotiate salary, although negotiating power can be limited for students and young professionals.

In short, when you get yourself to the interview through networking, you position yourself as someone who is more resourceful, committed, and connected than someone who simply could be applying to jobs at random online. That resourcefulness and focus also make you appear more valuable and make the company want you more. Want proof that this matters? I once negotiated a $50,000 increase in my *starting* salary because I knew the CEO of a company interviewing me. The chances of me being able to do that if I had landed the job interview after applying through a job board?

Zero.

Finally, the way you approach an employer initially also dictates how you will be treated after getting hired. Again, no organization will admit this to be true. However, if you get hired because you know a senior executive in the organization, you better believe you will be treated better than if you somehow manage to get hired without any personal/internal endorsements. Part of this will be subconscious, and part of this will be intentional.

## 7. It's Easier to Get a Job That Is Not Advertised Than a Job That Is Advertised

On the surface, this comment seems illogical, but it's absolutely true for a few reasons. First of all, if a job is promoted to the public, you are certainly not the only person who can see it or apply for it. When a job is advertised, an organization can receive hundreds of applications within a matter of hours. Some top employers even receive thousands of unsolicited résumés *every week*. Good luck standing out in a pile of 13,279 résumés. (On a side note, the best way to stand out in a stack of résumés is not to use keywords or a high-tech software program to beat a computer system's screening process. The best way to stand out in a stack of résumés is to never end up in the stack in the first place, as you will learn how to do in Chapters 5 and 6.)

Second, many publicly advertised jobs are *not currently available*. When you see an advertised job (regardless of where and how it is being promoted), it is often too late because the job has already been filled. There is no foolproof way to know, although the longer the job has been posted, the less likely it is still vacant. In some cases, employers just want to see who is out there, and they aren't 100 percent committed to or even that serious about hiring someone. Have you ever given online dating a try just to "see what's out there"? Employers engage in noncommittal scoping, too.

Last, most job openings are never publicly advertised to begin with; employers only promote a job opening to the public as a total last-ditch effort. Put yourself in the shoes of a hiring person for a second. Would you rather hire someone you found on Craigslist or someone you trust from your existing network? It's a no-brainer. When I worked for the Washington Wizards, HR would send a memo to the entire staff whenever a position became available. We could then talk to our supervisors about applying if we wanted to change jobs within the company, or we could refer people we knew. Jobs were frequently filled without needing to look outside the organization. Some companies even compensate their employees for helping them identify talent "behind the scenes." For example, my college roommate once played in a basketball league with a guy who tried to convince him to work for his company. We later learned that the guy would have gotten a $2,500 bonus if my friend had been hired through the referral.

## 8. It Is Easier to Get Your Dream Job Than Most Other Jobs

This comment probably sounds crazy as well, but it's also 100 percent true. You will be much more motivated during your job search if your goal is to get your "dream job" rather than if your goal is just to get "a job." Your motivation will lead to a more resourceful, positive mindset than if you just do what everyone else does and aim low. A better attitude will also make you more appealing as a job-seeker.

One reason I got a front-office job in the NBA at such a young age (while being ignored or rejected for other opportunities for which there was less competition) is because of how badly I wanted that NBA job. This burning desire oozed out of me when I was networking and when I was interviewing, and it made me a much more appealing candidate.

On the other hand, when I applied to jobs I randomly learned about through job boards or career fairs or on-campus recruiting, it was incredibly difficult for me to sell myself in a compelling manner. I had to fake my interest, and employers were not fooled. In hindsight, I'm *very* thankful those organizations blew me off! If they had hired me anyway, I probably would have ended up in a job I disliked.

Most people find job searches painful because they are going after the wrong jobs! When you are going after your dream job, your job search can actually be enjoyable (crazy thought, huh?) because of how excited you will be by what is waiting for you at the end of the tunnel. It is incredibly satisfying and empowering to go after your dreams with every ounce of your energy, and even more amazing when you reach your destination. Sadly, few people ever experience this phenomenon because they don't understand the relationship among desire, motivation, and performance. If you ever find yourself lacking motivation (during your job search or your career), it's probably because you are not aiming high enough.

Believe it or not, you are more likely to succeed when you aim high.

## 9. More Money Does Not Equal More Happiness— More Meaning Equals More Happiness

In May 2008, I left my dream job in the NBA. After five amazing seasons, I was ready for a new challenge, for something "even bigger." I made the mistake of thinking that more money was the answer, even though I was already making a six-figure salary.

One of my VIP clients with the Wizards was a very successful business owner, and he offered me a position to head up a new business development unit for his company. Without asking myself if the position was a good fit, I looked at the huge income potential and accepted the job.

Over the next 12 months, I worked for the best boss of my career, in the most supportive work environment you could imagine. My base salary was also four times higher than it was at the start of my career in the NBA just five years earlier. Sounds like a dream job, right?

Wrong. It was the least satisfying year of my entire career.

Don't misunderstand me. I'm not complaining. I am *extremely* grateful for the opportunity to have worked under great management while being compensated very generously. However, my tenure with that organization was incredibly unfulfilling because I was doing work that was not meaningful *to me*.

As a student or young professional, you may feel pressure to go after jobs with higher starting salaries, especially if you have hefty student loans or friends who *seem* to be cashing in. "Seem" is an important word in that last sentence. There are plenty of people who seem to have made it when, in reality, they are saddled with massive debt because they have purchased expensive cars and other toys they can't really afford.

All I can tell you is that the benefit of having a job you love is much more valuable than making a ton of money in a job you don't like. It certainly isn't a one-or-the-other proposition. I'm just recommending that you pursue your dreams first and worry about money later. The money will follow when you do great work. Even though people told me there was "no money in sports," I was making a six-figure salary by my third year in the NBA because I was so good at and passionate about my work. (Full disclosure: I had a sales job, so my income was connected to my performance.)

There's nothing wrong with wanting to make money. I want to make money, too. However, when you let money become the #1 motivator for your career decisions, you are asking for trouble.

## 10. Getting Your Dream Job Is a Competition, Not a Lottery

Guess what? You are not the only person who wants your dream job. Getting your dream job is simple, but it's not easy. It is going to require hard work on your part. You could be competing against hundreds or thousands of other people trying to break into or move up in the same organization or industry. I don't say that to scare you off. Instead, I say that to emphasize that you need to take your job search very seriously, and you need to be thinking at all times, *"What can I do to stand out in a good way from my competition?"*

When I worked in the NBA, people would tell me all the time how lucky I was to have gotten my dream job at such an early age. Most people didn't get it. There was nothing "lucky" about what happened to me. Even though I didn't realize it at the time, I was following a simple, six-step process you can follow to get your dream job as well. As mentioned in the introduction, the six steps are *Start, Identify, Makeover, Plan, Look,* and *Execute.*

No one came to me and delivered my dream job to my dorm room. I went out and got it. Similarly, if you want to get your dream job, *you* have to go out and get it. Getting your dream job is not the result of chance; it is the result of choice. If you have certain beliefs and if you take certain actions, you can get any job you want. Same thing goes for being successful after you get hired. You create your own "luck." Keep reading to learn how. . . .

## Austin Moyer Got His Dream Job with Polaris Industries

The long and strenuous path to my dream job started with networking in the spring of my junior year at a Baja SAE engineering design competition sponsored by Polaris Industries. While at the event, I noticed a pair of people standing nearby wearing Polaris shirts. Although my nerves were at an all-time high, I took a big step outside my comfort zone and struck up a conversation with them.

In our discussion, I learned a ton about what working for Polaris is truly like. The opportunity to design, fabricate, and test off-road vehicles (ORVs) sealed the deal. I knew this was the place for me!

I sent thank-you emails after the competition, and throughout the summer, I continued to sparingly email the employees I had met. September came around, and I submitted my online application. Several weeks later, I received a random phone call on a Wednesday afternoon. It turned into an hour-long phone interview. I wasn't prepared at all, but I felt the interview went very well, as I was able to discuss my ORV design and leadership experience through my four years in Baja SAE.

However, that Friday, I got an email from Polaris HR with heartbreaking news: I was no longer being considered for the position. I was devastated, but I was too persistent and passionate about the job to go down without a fight. Not sure of what to do next, I consulted Nancy Sheely, the university career services professional who had been a huge resource for me during my entire job search.

We decided that I would send an email to every Polaris agent I had ever met with this simple message: "I was very excited about this job and disappointed to no longer be a candidate for the position. What can I do to make myself more appealing to Polaris in the future?"

The following Wednesday, my phone lit up with a call from a Minnesota area code. Polaris had a spot open up, and they wanted to fly me in for interviews in two weeks!

After flying in, I had an afternoon of ORV rides, presentations, team-building activities, and a networking dinner in which I tried to be active, social, and sincere, but definitely not overbearing. The following morning was an exhausting process with four rounds of interviews in three hours.

For me, a huge key to my interviewing success was not only my preparation but also a 10-page project portfolio that helped me illustrate discussion points. I was able to leave a copy of this with each interviewer. Following my interviews, I spent every spare minute on planes and in hotels typing up 16 unique thank-you emails to each person I had met.

A week later, while visiting graduate schools, I received one of the best phone calls of my life: It was Polaris offering me a job.

I got my dream job and so can you!

—AUSTIN MOYER

# CHAPTER 2

# START

## (STEP #1)

> "Faith is taking the first step even when you don't see the whole staircase."
>
> —MARTIN LUTHER KING JR., CIVIL RIGHTS LEADER

## NO EMOTIONAL PAIN, NO GAIN

I could not get home from school fast enough to tell my Dad. After a great freshman season at Garden City High School, I had been invited to attend Camp Pontiac with the varsity basketball team. This was a big deal. Coach Martin rarely invited rising sophomores to play up with the varsity.

When Camp Pontiac finally arrived, I desperately wanted to fit in with my new teammates. At that point of my life, basketball was my #1 priority, so it was really important to me that I made a great first impression.

Shortly after my teammates and I arrived at Camp Pontiac, we had our first scrimmage. I don't remember the details of the game itself, but I will always remember what happened after the game.

I was seated under a tree with my teammates and our coaches. It was nearly 100 degrees outside, and we were all enjoying the shade. Given the temperature, most of us had our shirts off, including me. All of a sudden, one of my teammates looked at me and started to laugh hysterically. I was confused. No one had said anything funny. Then he pointed at me and said, "Look at Leibman. He's so puny you can see his heart beating!"

Several of the others chimed in: "Hey, you're right!" "Hey, look at that!" Next thing I knew, the entire team was having a good laugh at my expense. So were the coaches.

I looked down at my chest. Then I thought to myself: *"Wow, I never noticed that before. You actually can see my heart beating."* However, I didn't want to agree with them so I replied, "You guys are crazy. I don't know what you're talking about."

At the time, I was 5'10" and 119 pounds, so I knew I didn't have the body of a Greek god. However, I hadn't realized how obvious my physical weakness was to others. It felt like my manhood had just been questioned by my peers, a tough pill to swallow for a shy 15-year-old kid.

That night, when none of my teammates were around, I went into the bathroom and just stared at myself in the mirror shirtless. I hated what I saw. After feeling sorry for myself for a few minutes, I realized I had only two options: *do nothing* or *do something*. I vowed that no one would ever be able to make fun of my body again.

When I returned home the following week, I joined a local health club. Completely baffled on how to use any of the machines or weights, I was able to get some help from an older friend of mine, John, who had played professional basketball in Europe. The first time John took me to the weight room with him, I struggled to bench press a 45-pound bar. If you are not a weightlifter, let's just say my 89-year-old Grandma could probably do that without breaking a sweat. Needless to say, my entry into weightlifting was not easy or very impressive. However, I was absolutely committed to changing my body. I never wanted to feel like I did that day at Camp Pontiac ever again.

So I persisted. Slowly, I made progress. Month by month, I got a little stronger, a little bigger, and a little more confident.

Fast-forward to the following summer. I was playing basketball with John, whom I had not seen for six months. We were sitting down during a break, and I was shirtless. Out of nowhere, he looked at me and laughed. Immediately, I flashed back to the summer before, but John said something that was completely different from what my teammate had said just one year earlier: "Leibman, you been taking steroids or something? Your chest is huge."

I looked down at my chest, and I couldn't see my heart beating anymore. I replied, "Nope. Just been hitting the gym." Apparently, all the hours in the weight room over the last year had paid off. (In case you are wondering, my growth was all natural.) When I think back to the day my body was publicly mocked, I realize now what a gift that experience ultimately was. Had my teammate not embarrassed me in front of my peers, I would never have been motivated to redesign my body.

That painful experience was the impetus for so much good in my life. Today, I am 6'1" and 185 pounds with less than 10 percent body fat. While no one is ever going to confuse me with an NFL linebacker, and while some people still call me skinny (which I *hate* to be called, for the record), I have muscles in places that I didn't know you could build muscles in when I was a teenager. That embarrassing incident ultimately helped me develop greater confidence and a passion for fitness that has enabled me to help other people change their bodies and lives as well.

> LEIBMAN LIFE LESSON:
> *Just because you don't like where you are today does not mean you have to be there tomorrow.*

I have realized that my most painful moments or periods were all blessings in disguise because they made me so uncomfortable that I was inspired to *do something*. Short-term pain is needed to create long-term change

I share this story with you because most people don't read job-search books for fun. As a result, I have to assume you picked up this book because of some sort of "pain" in your life. Perhaps you are having trouble landing your first real job after college, perhaps you feel like you are having a quarter-life crisis in a dead-end job, or perhaps you got laid off for no apparent reason.

Embrace the pain and use it to fuel your fire. Pain is the best motivator there is.

# DON'T MAKE EXCUSES

I was watching the news one day in 2010, and a 21-year-old college graduate was complaining about how "hard it is to get a job in this economy." However, he made no mention of what he had done to get a job or what he was doing to change his situation. How many hours was he devoting to his job search each day? How many professional networking events had he attended over the last six months? How many people had he asked for advice? How much time had he spent on LinkedIn and other online networking channels? How many books, blogs, or other resources had he read to make sure he was presenting himself as professionally as possible?

Winners don't whine, and whiners don't win.

In order to get your dream job (or achieve any goal), you need to take full, 100 percent accountability for making it happen. If you are not satisfied with where your career is right now, you have only two choices (as I did when my teammates at Camp Pontiac made fun of my body): *do nothing* or *do something*. Since you are reading this book, I know you want to do something, so I'll emphasize this point very quickly. No one is going to come to you and rescue you from your career doldrums and hand you your dream job in a gift basket. The only person who can make it happen is *you*.

You don't need to know what your dream job is yet. You don't need to know how to get your dream job. You don't even need to be fully convinced you can get your dream job. You just need to be willing to start and take charge of steering your career where you want it to go. Along those lines, let's destroy five common excuses for not starting.

## Excuse #1: The Economy

You don't need me to bombard you with stats about how bad the recession is. The media has already done more than enough of that. I'll just say this:

Take a look at national unemployment data from the Bureau of Labor Statistics over the last 50 years or so. You will see that unemployment has always fluctuated up and down with peaks in the 8–10 percent range (where it was in 2011) versus valleys in the 2–4 percent range. Where will it be in the next few years? Who knows?

More important, who cares? Let me state the obvious since so many people seem to be missing it: How many jobs do you need to get?

One job! Not 100 jobs. Not 25 jobs. Not even three jobs. You just need one job. That's it.

There is absolutely nothing you could say that could convince me that you have a legitimate reason to be worried about getting your dream job because of a down economy. I shared this philosophy with one of my mentors, who encouraged me to tone down my stance for fear of offending some people—but I won't. The economy is only a problem if you think it's a problem. Don't worry about unemployment statistics. Don't allow yourself to be brainwashed into a state of fear by the media. When I was a senior in college, unemployment was the highest it had been in 10 years. That didn't stop me from landing my dream job.

> **LEIBMAN LIFE LESSON:**
> *The economy does not matter.*
> *You need just one job.*

## Excuse #2: Youth or Lack of Experience

Did you ever have a lemonade stand when you were little? As kids, my brother and I would have lemonade stands every summer as a way to make extra cash. We would set up a table and chairs on the corner of the street we lived on in the suburbs of Long Island, N.Y., and people would always stop and buy our lemonade.

Did people stop because of a thirst that needed to be quenched at that very moment? Of course not! Instead, people stopped because of something I call *The Lemonade Stand Principle*, which states that older people like to help younger people who are ambitious and enthusiastic. I have found this to be true as a 9-year-old kid selling lemonade, as a 21-year-old student trying to break into pro sports, as a 26-year-old career-changer, and as a 27-year-old entrepreneur starting his own business.

Enthusiasm is contagious, and genuine ambition is inspiring. When my brother and I had our lemonade stands, we would be out there with signs, trying to wave down every car that passed by. Our enthusiasm inspired people to want to help us.

Similarly, most older executives *love* young "go-getters" because they remind them of themselves. When older executives look at you (assuming you have a winning attitude), they see whom they were 20, 30, or 40 years ago. They remember the challenges they went through, and they remember how someone helped them get started. Do not make the mistake of thinking that people won't want to help you. When you approach people the right way, you will be amazed at who will support you, just like I was when I looked for a job as a student. Your youth is a tremendous advantage that you should not feel guilty about utilizing. In 10 to 20 years, you can return the favor to a younger person when you are the successful senior executive.

> **LEIBMAN LIFE LESSON:**
> *Youth is not an obstacle. Youth is a huge advantage for your career.* Remember The Lemonade Stand Principle.

If you have already graduated from college, you can still benefit from *The Lemonade Stand Principle*, although it will never be as easy to get career advice and support as it is while you are a student. An optimistic attitude is essential throughout your job search, and it is one of the traits that can overcome deficiencies in your résumé. If you are feeling defeated and frustrated and are conveying those emotions to others, you need to stop yourself right now! You have to get excited first before you can expect others to get excited about helping you. An enthusiastic attitude will keep you optimistic and resilient.

## Excuse #3: Pedigree or Credentials

As I mentioned earlier, I interviewed with the Washington Wizards for an internship position at the end of my junior year in college, and I got rejected. When that happened, I initially told myself that I must not have been good enough to get a job in the NBA. At the time, I assumed that the entire organization was surely composed of Ivy League graduates with 4.0 GPAs. An NBA team receiving hundreds of résumés each week would certainly hire only the smartest, most qualified candidates, right?

Not even close.

Here is what I learned after getting hired by the Wizards. Many of the organization's employees went to community colleges or colleges I had never heard of, and some of the most senior executives did not even go to college. Most of the team's employees simply got hired because of their attitude or personality or because they knew how to conduct a job search. They were definitely not hired because of their pedigrees. In addition, there were men and women of all ages, races, and backgrounds in the company. Employers value diversity.

Here's the inside scoop. Employers hire candidates they know, like, and trust or candidates endorsed by people they know, like, and trust. As a result, the most qualified people are not always the ones to get hired. Credentials are overrated. Intangibles and endorsements are underrated. This is especially true when you are a student or young professional.

This is not meant to give you an excuse for not maintaining a high GPA, doing internships, and being proactive if you are still a student. Is it easier for a Harvard grad with a 4.0 GPA to get a job than someone with 2.1 GPA from a community college? Absolutely. My point is this: Don't use your lack of pedigree or credentials as an excuse for why you can't break into a certain organization or industry. Your major doesn't matter either. Great employers are more interested in skill sets and personality traits than what it says on your diploma.

> **LEIBMAN LIFE LESSON:**
>
> *The most qualified person is not always the one who gets hired. There is someone with a weaker pedigree than you who has your dream job right now.*

## Excuse #4: Time

If you think you don't have the time to go after your dream job, here is what I want you to do. For one full week (Monday morning through Sunday night), keep a journal of how you spend every single minute of your time. If you are like most people, you will probably find at least 15 to 20 hours (some people find much more) spent on useless activities like watching TV, playing video games, or hanging out in your house by yourself. If you use your time wisely, you will have more than enough time right now to go after your dream job.

## Excuse #5: Fear

What are you afraid of? Are you afraid of people rejecting you? Are you afraid of not succeeding? Are you afraid of the unknown?

Guess what? All people who have ever pursued their dreams were afraid at the start as well! I was really nervous going to networking events in college, but I did it anyway. I was terrified about starting my own business in 2009, but I did it anyway. Everything gets much easier with practice. Fear is not a legitimate reason for not trying. It is normal to be afraid. That's a sign you are on to something big. If you don't have any fear, you are not aiming high enough. Just start. With action, the fear will disappear. You have been through unfamiliar situations before, like when you started college. You can do it again.

## EXPECT DOUBTERS AND USE THEM TO FUEL YOUR FIRE

Whenever you try to do something big or try to do something for the first time, people will doubt you. Do not be surprised when this happens. This is the byproduct of most people aiming way too low with how they live their lives. More specifically, there are five main reasons why people will doubt that you can achieve your dreams.

1. *They think they are helping you.* This happens often with our family and closest friends. When I was a student, one of my family members told me I should be "more realistic" when it came to my first job out of college. Even though this bothered me, I knew her heart was in the right place. She thought she was doing me a favor by not letting me get my hopes up only to be disappointed (since she thought I would fail).

2. *They don't believe they could succeed at what you are trying to do.* Another reason people will doubt you is because they don't believe they could do what you are trying to achieve, either because they tried and gave up or because they never tried. Several years ago, I went to lunch with a group of professional speakers who were much older than me. During our meal, I shared my dream of publishing a book. Immediately, the entire group shared their stories of being unable to get a publisher to offer them a book deal, and a few of them implied that it would be impossible for me to publish a book "at this stage of my career." Let me emphasize one point: I was at lunch with a group of *motivational* speakers. These people are supposed to inspire others for a living, and they were shooting down my dream! Since I ultimately made it happen, I think this is actually pretty ironic and humorous. Anyway, the message is this: Most people (even some motivational speakers) have allowed life to beat them down. Never allow someone else's failures, insecurity, or lack of faith to dictate whether you believe *your* dreams are possible.

3. *You are trying to succeed faster than they did.* Other people might doubt you because they make the mistake of thinking that it's not possible for someone else to get somewhere sooner than they did. When I was a senior in college, I shared my dream of working in pro sports with a senior executive from an NFL team. He had been unable to get a job in sports right after college, so he told me it would be impossible for me to

do it. He then suggested I get experience in another industry and consider applying for jobs in sports five to 10 years later. (This is an example of one of the terrible pieces of advice given to me as a young professional.)

4. *They don't like your dream.* Don't expect all of your friends or family members to be excited about your vision. I don't know your particular situation, so all I will say is that when you reach adulthood, it's time to make your own decisions. One of the biggest recipes for unhappiness is to bury your dreams in order to make other people happy. As long as your dream does not hurt you or anyone else, then go after it with everything you have.

5. *Some people actually don't want you to succeed.* This is also known as being a "hater." Yes, this sounds jaded, but it's true. Some people incorrectly believe that there is a finite supply of happiness or success available in the world. As a result, they think that if you are happy or successful, it somehow makes it less likely for them to be. The truth is that there is an *infinite* supply of success and happiness available to anyone willing to put in the necessary effort.

The overall message is this: Do not expect everyone to support your dreams unconditionally. Instead, when you encounter doubters, use their doubts or criticism as added motivation. In a way, I got my first dream job (to become an NBA executive) and my second dream job (to become a published author) *because* people doubted me, not in spite of people doubting me. I used doubts from other people to ignite my conviction that I would succeed. Doubters made me want it more and gave me an "enemy" to fight against. The challenges unleashed my competitive juices and my desire to win. I learned at an early age that your ultimate success has nothing to do with what other people think about your dreams. Your success or failure will

> LEIBMAN LIFE LESSON:
>
> *When someone doubts your dream, he has actually done you a favor.*

be the result of how you *respond* to fear, what you tell yourself is possible, and the subsequent actions you are willing to take to make your dreams a reality.

## JOB SEARCH Q&A WITH THE AUTHOR

Here are answers to some common questions from job-seekers as they think about starting job searches.

**Q:** I'm still in college. What can I do now to make it easier to get my dream job when I graduate?

**A:** First of all, as a general rule, keep your GPA over 3.0 because employers will make assumptions about your work ethic and intelligence based on your GPA. (You can overcome a lower GPA, but why make this process harder than it needs to be?) In addition to taking your classes seriously, get as much experience as possible. This could include leadership experience, volunteer experience, internship experience, or experience traveling/studying abroad in a foreign country. You should also prioritize relationship-building with professors, alumni, your campus career center, and other contacts on and off campus.

**Q:** I'm not sure what I want to do next. Should I just go to grad school?

**A:** While I am a huge advocate for education, I believe it's a mistake to go to grad school to "figure things out" (I almost did that a few years ago) or just because you think the economy is down. I have many friends who went to grad school right after college, only to end up in careers completely unrelated to the subject of their advanced degrees. Years later, they are still paying off their student loans. The investment of time and money is significant, so if you are going to go to grad school, you better have strong evidence that it will benefit a specific career path that you are following. If you decide that grad school makes sense for you, check out www.DarrellBennett.com for tips from a Harvard Law School alumnus, Darrell Bennett, on how to get into any grad school you want.

**Q:** I'm employed, but I can't take it at my job anymore! Is there any problem with quitting so that I can devote all my time to looking for my next job?

**A:** I'd really encourage you to stick it out. There is definitely a bias against unemployed job candidates, and it's nice to have a steady paycheck as you look for your next job. Assuming you stay at your job, here are three pieces of advice for you:

▶ *Keep your job search 100 percent separate from your current job.* Your employer has the right and the ability to monitor any of your email/Internet activities. When communicating with potential employers and networking contacts, use a personal email address, personal home address, personal cell phone number, and so on.

▶ *Publicize your job search carefully.* Be careful whom you tell about your job search and what you post online. Tell only friends, family, and colleagues whom you really trust. Be particularly careful with colleagues because people love to gossip at work, and word travels fast when an employee is looking to leave.

▶ *Keep giving your best effort at your current job.* Getting fired won't help your cause in getting a new job, so don't do anything at work to draw negative attention to yourself.

**Q:** I'm unemployed. Will employers hold this against me, and what can I do to make myself more marketable?

**A:** Employers won't usually admit this, and it might not be fair, but there is a huge bias against candidates who are unemployed. The longer you are out of work, the less valuable you appear. The implication is "If this person is so great, how come no one has hired her?"

One of the first questions people ask at any event (personal or professional) is "So, what do you do?" Other than saying you are a taxidermist, there is nothing worse than having to respond, "Well, I'm unemployed." One of the first questions employers ask you in an interview when learning you are out of work is "So, what have you been doing to stay busy during your unemployment?" Other than saying, "Watching every season of *Survivor*," there is nothing worse you could say than "conducting a job search."

Regardless of why you are unemployed, donate some of your time to a professional association connected to your field or an organization with some name recognition. Try to find an organization where you can utilize skills related to your career. For example, if you are looking for a job in sales or marketing, look for an organization you can support with marketing or fund-raising. Then, when someone asks what you do or what you have been doing to stay busy, you can respond with something like, "I've been helping ABC Nonprofit Organization with their fund-raising, while considering a career change." Another idea would be to enroll in a professional development course at a community college or library where you can enhance skills/knowledge related to your career.

## START NOW

When people ask me what I do, my current response is "I help young professionals get their dream jobs." Regardless of the person's age, I am almost always met with something like, "Wow, I wish I met you when I was in college."

It's never too late to change directions, but the best time to go after your dream job is now, when you are young and hungry.

Next week becomes next month becomes next year becomes never. Don't fool yourself into thinking that you will be better off going after your dream job in the future. *Now* is always the best time.

**Circumstances will never be perfect, so stop waiting.
Start *now*!**

## *Joseph Speziale Got His Dream Job with Microsoft*

It all started six months before I was about to graduate. I was winding down my senior year at the University of South Florida, and I started thinking about what I wanted to do and where I wanted to work. As an MIS major, working at four companies stuck out as dream jobs: Apple, Google, Facebook, and Microsoft. As I was weighing the pros and cons of each, I couldn't help but think it was still a long shot for a guy like me at a non–Ivy League school to make it into one of those companies right out of college. Nonetheless, I was willing to start the process and see what happened.

After much research, I decided that I wanted to work for Microsoft because of the company culture and emphasis on innovation. I felt that I could be a huge asset because of my drive and my longing to make a big difference in the IT world. I applied for a position on Microsoft's website. Months went by without a response, and I started to feel like my only options were smaller IT firms. I almost gave up.

Then, one month before graduation, I learned that Microsoft would be on campus on a Saturday morning to do an information session about potential jobs after graduation. I was very excited about that news and couldn't wait to go.

When Saturday finally came, I was tired and sick. I woke my friend up, and I asked him if he thought I should go anyway. He said, "This is your future and it's Microsoft. Just go!" I took his advice and struggled out of bed and made it to the information session. I was turned off upon arrival by the fact that there were more than 150 people there and only one recruiter, but the presentation brought my excitement back.

Throughout the presentation, I thought to myself, "How am I going to stand out from everyone else?" I decided to get the recruiter's email. The second I got home, I wrote a two-page email to her about why I should be hired and why I wanted to work for Microsoft.

She responded and told me that she would pass my résumé along to the right people. Within weeks, I received an email from Microsoft to set up a phone interview. This was the one chance I'd waited for my whole life, so I stressed, studied, and researched until the day came. I was so nervous I couldn't sleep the night before. The interview came and went and I couldn't help but feel extremely confident about my responses and the dialogue I had with the recruiter. Within two weeks, Microsoft invited me up to Charlotte for face-to-face interviews. At that point, I could taste it and was ready to make a lasting impression on every person who interviewed me. After the in-person interviews, the wait for a response seemed like years, but after two long weeks, I received my offer from Microsoft.

I got my dream job and so can you!

—JOSEPH SPEZIALE

# CHAPTER 3

# IDENTIFY

## (STEP #2)

> "One reason so few of us achieve what we truly want is that
> we never direct our focus; we never concentrate our power."
>
> —ANTHONY ROBBINS, AUTHOR OF *UNLIMITED POWER*

October 19, 1996: in New Hyde Park, N.Y. (at a bagel shop)

"Pete, stop arguing with me and just try to get 20," my father pleaded with me on the afternoon before one of my high school games.

"Dad, I've never scored more than 12 points in a basketball game. How am I going to get 20?" I argued back.

My father continued: "You are hurting yourself as a player and hurting the team by being so passive on the court. For tonight only, I want you to try to score at least 20 points. I don't care how many assists you get. I don't care how many rebounds you get. I don't care how many turnovers you make. I don't even care if the team wins. Just get 20. That is your one goal for tonight's game. The only reason you have never scored 20 points before is because you have never set a goal to score 20 points in a game."

"OK. I'll try," I replied hesitantly.

Five hours later, I went out and scored 24 points. We also won the game easily. Did that happen because I had suddenly become a better player in a matter of hours? Of course not. I scored more than 20 points for the first time in my life because I was open-minded and because I was focused on one clear goal.

My Dad did not tell me to get 20 points *or* 15 assists *or* 10 rebounds *or* seven steals *or* five blocks. Because he gave me one clear target, I was able to do something I had never done before, an achievement I had previously thought was impossible.

The incredible power of focus. . . .

You can burn a hole through an object if you hold a magnifying glass between the object and the sun long enough. However, the magnifying glass loses all its power if you start waving it all over the place. Most job-seekers make an analogous mistake. They put their eggs in 178 different baskets.

My goal in college was not to work for a pro sports franchise like the Washington Wizards *or* a federal agency like the CIA *or* a Big 4 accounting firm like Ernst & Young *or* a computer technology company like Microsoft *or* a top nonprofit organization like the American Cancer Society. I wanted a marketing/sales job with a pro sports franchise in Washington, D.C., or Baltimore. Period.

> LEIBMAN LIFE LESSON:
> *You help yourself when you are less flexible, so don't pursue every possible opportunity. Focus will help you achieve your goal faster.*

The #1 objective of this chapter is to help you develop focus and commitment for your job search, so that you can get your dream job faster and with less effort. This chapter will start with do's and don'ts for identifying what your dream job is. Then, you will also learn the following:

► How to identify your passions, talents, and values (the "big picture" of what you want from your career)

► How to identify your *Dream Job Description* (the details of what you want from your career)

► How to identify your *Target Market* (a list of your ideal employers)

Do not be overwhelmed by all the self-assessment questions in this chapter. They are designed to help you brainstorm ideas and then to help you drill deeper. Some questions will resonate with you more than others. Take your time when answering them.

## WHAT IS A DREAM JOB?

I get a lot of interesting reactions when I tell people that I help young professionals get their dream jobs. Cynics say, "Dream jobs don't exist." Pessimists say, "You can't get your dream job in this economy." And some people think I can help them find a job where they can earn a six-figure salary to sit on the beach and drink Coronas all day.

Most people misunderstand what I mean, so here is my definition of a dream job:

> "A *dream job* is a job that combines your talents and passions in a way that is meaningful *to you*."

If you want to get your dream job, you need to determine what you are good at and what you love to do. Then, you need to combine those talents and passions in a way that excites you and matters to you. Sounds simple enough, right? Well, most people don't know how to do it.

Most people spend more time working on their résumé than they do deciding what type of job they actually want! You have virtually no chance of ending up in your dream job unless you identify what it is *before* you start your job search. If you don't have a destination in mind, you will probably end up somewhere you don't really want to be. Be patient with yourself. Here are seven do's and don'ts for identifying your dream job.

1. *Don't pursue other people's dreams.* Everyone loves to give career advice to students and young professionals, so it's easy to get brainwashed and pursue a job for the wrong reasons. You won't find your dream job by chasing a hot industry or

field or by naively accepting "advice" being jammed down your throat by parents, family, friends, professors, or society. The only way to get your dream job is to be honest about what *you* want to do. The answer is inside you, not outside.

2. *Don't expect perfection.* A dream job is not a soul mate. It's not about finding "the one." There are lots of jobs out there that could be dream jobs for you. A dream job is also not a perfect job. When I had my first dream job working for an NBA team, there were still plenty of times when I got frustrated or when I fantasized about doing something else. In my second dream job as a speaker, author, career coach, and entrepreneur, I also have moments when I experience stress and challenges. This is normal when you try to do big things. No job will ever be perfect, exciting, and free from frustration 100 percent of the time. If that is your expectation, you will always be disappointed.

3. *Don't put too much pressure on yourself.* If you end up pursuing a career that doesn't work for you, you can change directions at any time. Make your career decisions carefully, but understand that your next job will probably not be a job you will have for the rest of your life. In fact, most people change jobs (and careers) a number of times throughout their lives.

4. *Try new things.* The best way to find out what you like to do and what you are good at is through personal experience. This is why it's important to take a variety of courses, travel to new places, read about different subjects, volunteer, intern, and so on. Put yourself in as many different environments as possible. The more you experience in college and as a young professional, the easier it will be to determine what you want from your career.

5. *Take some tests.* Career assessments might confirm what you already know, or they might shed light on your talents and passions if you are struggling to identify them on your own. Check with your college's career center to see what options

are available. Most career centers offer free career testing to students, and many offer lifetime assistance to alumni as well. It amazes me how few students and young professionals utilize their college's career center. At the minimum, your college's career center or alumni association should be able to direct you to resources to use on your own. There are two caveats on this, however. Don't automatically assume that you have to do what a career test thinks you should do, and don't limit your thinking to the results from a career assessment.

6. *Talk to people you trust.* Find several people you trust, and ask for their help in brainstorming potential career paths for you based on what they consider your strengths to be. While you need to come to your own conclusions, talking out loud to people you respect can uncover ideas you had not previously considered. It's also highly recommended to talk to people in any fields of interest. (This is referred to as an Informational Interview.) There are all sorts of opportunities that you don't even know about right now, and you also want to know as much as possible about a career before you pursue it.

7. *Talk to yourself.* If you don't know what your passions and talents are, you need to start paying more attention to how you feel as you live your life. When was the last time you went somewhere peaceful by yourself to think about what you want out of life? Most people have *never* taken time to do this, and that's why they end up in places they don't want to be. As a result, let's spend some time on this strategy.

## THE RIGHT QUESTIONS WILL PRODUCE THE RIGHT ANSWERS

I truly believe that your dreams are buried inside you right now. You might not be aware of what's really going on in your head, since fear of rejection and fear of failure usually get in the way and prevent us from being honest about what our true dreams are. However, you were born with special gifts and innate interests, and your experiences have shaped your passions, talents, and values.

A great way to unlock the "mystery" of what you truly want from your life is to ask yourself a series of very strategic questions. Don't ask yourself self-defeating questions like "What's wrong with me?" or "How did I get myself in this position?" or "Why can't I figure out what I want to do?" Instead, ask yourself questions that empower you.

The questions presented in the following pages will help you get to the core of who you really are and what you really want. Even if you think you already know what your dream job is, go through these sections slowly. The better you understand yourself, the easier it will be to determine what your dream job is and what you really want out of your life.

If you try to go through the next few sections in a span of three minutes (e.g., during a commercial break of *Jersey Shore*), these exercises will be meaningless! These are very profound questions, so go somewhere peaceful outside where you will be able to think clearly. If that sounds like too much work, consider this: *Isn't it worth taking the time to design the life of your dreams?*

I tend to do my best thinking when I am outside in nature because I'm relaxed and inspired by the beauty surrounding me. This could be at a pond, at a lake, at a beach, in the woods, or near a mountain. If a scenic, outdoor location is not easily accessible, just find a field and lay on your back and stare up at the sky as you think. If you live in North Dakota and it's January and 20 degrees below 0 outside, then just go somewhere where you can *look* outside! Bottom line: It's hard to think outside the box when you are in a room that is the size of a box, so go somewhere where you will be inspired to *think big*.

The goal for these questions, which I refer to as "The Sweet 16," is to help you identify your passions, talents, and values, so that you can get some ideas for industries and job functions that are of interest to you. There is no single question or exercise that will automatically help you figure out what you want from your career and your life. As previously stated, some of the questions in this chapter should resonate with you more than others, and these are certainly not the only questions you should be asking yourself. As I have experienced, your dreams will also evolve over time, so make sure to ask yourself these questions on a regular basis. The result will be a much more satisfying career . . . and a much better life!

## Start with the Big Picture

▶ *Let's assume you have the ability to create your ideal life. What would your life look like in five years?*

If you have never asked yourself this question, be prepared to spend some time thinking through your answer very carefully. It will be worth it. If you are not sure where to begin (many people are not), think about what you want to *have* in the future, who you want to *be* in the future, and where you want to *live* in the future. This question is important because your work is just one piece of the puzzle. You have to identify what you want from your *life* before you identify what you want from your career. Most people pursue a career first, and then try to build their life around that career. It doesn't work that way.

Last point on this question: When you identify what you want from your life, ask yourself *why* you want what you do, and be honest. For example, if you want a Lamborghini, are you really after a Lamborghini because of its quality as a vehicle, or because of what you think having a Lamborghini will do for your life? This leads us to the next question.

▶ *What is your definition of success?*

In today's media-driven world, it's easy to be brainwashed and to lose track of what really matters to you. Many young professionals achieve "success." This can happen when you make career decisions based on what you think other people will be impressed by. I fell prey to the trap of pursuing society's definition of success in 2008 when I decided to leave

> LEIBMAN LIFE LESSON:
>
> *If you are not honest or clear about what you want from your life and what success means to you, you will never feel successful, no matter how much you achieve or acquire.*

my front-office job in the NBA. I was ready for a new challenge, and I wanted to do something "bigger." However, I made the mistake of thinking that any job where I could make even more money would make me feel even happier and more successful. I was wrong. What I ultimately realized was that my definition of success included service, creativity, and influence. That's why I eventually pursued a career as a speaker and author. Make sure you know what success means to you, and then pursue a career where you can achieve it.

► *What are your five proudest achievements, and why do these achievements mean so much to you?*

When you answer this question, your deepest values will usually surface. For example, one of my proudest achievements at the start of my career after college was the creation of an annual event called The Washington Wizards' Sports Careers Day (which I'll talk about a little more in Chapter 10). I was really proud of the event because of the impact it made on the franchise and on the lives of the thousands of students who participated. The sense of pride I felt for this event was a clue that helped me identify my second dream job because I realized that creativity and influence were two values I would need to feel fulfilled in my career.

## Consider the End

► *If you found out that you had only 12 months left to live and you had to work every day, what would you do?*

This might sound like a morbid or bizarre question, but it cuts right to the core of what you are most passionate about and what you really want from your work. Life is so precious, but most people take it for granted, especially students and young professionals. You have your entire life ahead of you, but nothing is guaranteed. You don't know what the future holds. "Next year" can turn into "never" pretty quickly. Don't fool yourself into thinking that you will go after your dreams later in life. *Now is always the best time to go after your dreams.*

► *What do you want people to say about you after you die?*

Again, this might sound like a strange, dark question for a student or young professional to ask herself. You may be thinking, "C'mon, Pete! I have my entire life ahead of me. Chill out!" However, thinking about the legacy you want to leave behind is a great way to identify your values, while at the same time clarifying the impact you want to have through your work. Again, by not identifying your values, you'll be much more likely to end up in a career that feels meaningless and unsatisfying. Most people wait until they are 70 years old to think

> LEIBMAN LIFE LESSON:
> *Not sure what you want to do? Identify the people you admire most, and pursue a career where you can have a similar or even larger impact on the world.*

about their legacy. At that point of your life, your legacy will already be fairly well defined. Think of the tremendous legacy you could build by planning for it from the start of your career.

## Think Big

► *Whom do you admire most and why?*

As a child, you likely had some heroes. What about now? Most people stop looking for role models once they reach the age of 18, as if it's inappropriate to look up to people once you are no longer a minor. It is *not* inappropriate.

The answer to this question will tell you a lot about your values. If your answer is Donald Trump, you probably have different dreams from someone whose answer is Mother Teresa. This is not to imply that The Donald has not made a tremendously positive impact on the world; he's just done it in a very different way than Mother Teresa has.

There are no right or wrong answers here. Some people are born to be business titans, and some people are born to be humanitarians. If you feel strongly about your answer to this question, what about pursuing a career on the path to becoming the person you admire the most or exceeding what that person has achieved?

A couple of notes on this question. First, don't just look at famous people. Whom do you admire most among the people you know, and what do you admire most about them?

Second, understand that your heroes will change as you get older. Like many kids, when I was little, Michael Jordan was my hero. I wanted to "be like Mike," so playing basketball was my passion as a child and teenager. By my mid-20s, my heroes had become personal/professional development gurus like Anthony Robbins, Brian Tracy, Jack Canfield, and Stephen Covey, which is why I ultimately pursued a career as a speaker and author.

► *If you could be the best in the world at anything, what would it be?*

We all desire to reach our full potential, and we all have unique, inborn gifts. Most people settle for being just average at something they were not born to do, rather than understanding that there is *something* at which they could be world-class. Pursue a career where you will want to achieve mastery. Becoming an expert is very satisfying (and lucrative), and expertise is transferrable across organizations and industries.

► *If you had the ability to change anything about the world (or to help any group of people), what would you do, and why?*

We all want to make a difference in the world somehow, but most people don't realize that they actually can make a difference through their work. Find some problem that you want to solve or a group of people you want to help. Then, consider careers that will enable you to be part of the solution for the problem you identified. When you do that, you will never have a day at work when you will lack motivation. And remember that nonprofits are not the only organizations that make the world a better place. For-profit corporations solve problems and improve the world, too.

## Ignore Money and Fear

► *What would you do if every job paid the same salary?*

► *What type of job would you pursue if you knew you would get it and if you knew you would succeed after getting hired?*

If you can take money and fear out of the equation, you will be much more likely to home in on what you truly want to do. Based on societal pressures, we overestimate the importance of money. Fear of failure often prevents us from pursuing our dreams. Warning: It is not possible to be completely happy if you have a dream that you keep buried for any reason! Never let fear prevent you from trying. Not trying is the only real failure.

## Embrace Pain and Struggle

► *What personal struggles or challenges have you or your closest friends/family members overcome?*

If you went through a personal challenge, others surely have as well. There are probably a lot of other people right now who desperately need to know how you overcame your struggle. In fact, this is a main reason why I wrote this book. I went through challenges starting my career and then again when I reinvented myself in my mid to late 20s. Now, I derive great satisfaction out of using my experiences to help other people overcome similar obstacles. Look for careers where you can help others attain the success you have achieved in your life. It is very empowering and meaningful to help people through a problem you have overcome firsthand.

In addition to dealing with personal challenges, you have surely seen family or friends struggle as well. What about using what you learned through the process to prevent other people from experiencing a similar type of pain? For example, I know someone whose sister was raped when she was in college. Now, this man's professional mission is to prevent other families from experiencing the pain his family went through, so he travels the country speaking to groups about sexual assault. Most people would not think of this as a dream job, but he derives great satisfaction and meaning from his incredibly important work, and he is having an amazing impact on the world.

Note: If the experience you or a close one went through is too painful for you to be reminded of on a daily basis, you should seek professional help with the issue, and you certainly don't have to devote your career to helping others in that area. It's just an idea to consider.

## Probe for Your Passions and Talents

► *What activities do you enjoy participating in during your free time, and are there any common elements among those activities?*

Your personal hobbies and passions can often be turned into a dream job. I took my passion for sports and my passion for business and turned them into a career in sports marketing after college. I also have a tremendous passion for knowledge and education, and I was able to build a career from that as a speaker and author at the end of my 20s.

Having said that, I must add that you should be careful not to assume that any job related to your hobbies will be a dream job. One of my primary hobbies is exercising, and I also run some sports conditioning classes for groups in my free time. However, I would go out of my mind if I had to train clients in a gym as a full-time job. It's something I enjoy doing *in moderation.*

Before trying to turn a hobby into a full-time career, consider if it's something you would want to spend 40 to 50 hours a week doing. It's also worth noting that your career can consist of multiple jobs, as mine does now. I have my primary career as a speaker, career coach, and author, but I also run several boot camp classes a week as a job "on the side." You could also start a small part-time business related to one of your hobbies, as we'll talk about in Chapter 13.

► *What are you doing when you are happiest and most confident, and are there any common elements among those times?*

After identifying times when you are happiest and most confident, try to identify if there are any common elements. This can give you insight into your ideal work environment or job function.

Again, just make sure to ask yourself if you would want to be in that environment for 40 to 50 hours a week.

You could also explore careers where you could help other people feel like you do during your happiest times. For example, when I think back to my childhood, my happiest times were spent playing basketball with friends and with my Dad. When I worked in the NBA, I derived great satisfaction from my job because I helped other kids and families have memorable experiences related to basketball.

► *If you had to read 100 books in 100 days on one topic, what one topic would you read about, and why?*

If you can identify a topic that you would want to study in-depth for 100 straight days, you have probably identified a subject that is a passion. What about pursuing a career related to that topic?

► *What is easy for you that might not be easy for others?*

► *What skills or talents do people often compliment you on?*

It's very easy for us to take our strengths for granted. Most people, myself included, are much better at listing their weaknesses and flaws than at listing their talents. When I worked for the Washington Wizards, one of my colleagues told me I had a gift for public speaking after I served as emcee for The Washington Wizards' Sports Careers Day in 2007. Somehow, it did not even cross my mind at the time that being able to speak confidently in front of a group of 5,000 people was a big deal! Ask people you trust for help in identifying your strengths. Your talents are often more noticeable to the people around you than they are to you.

> LEIBMAN LIFE LESSON:
> *When you get to utilize your strengths on a daily basis at work, you will be much happier, and your performance will skyrocket.*

## CREATE YOUR OWN DREAM JOB DESCRIPTION

After you have spent some time thinking about the big picture, you need to drill deeper and create your Dream Job Description (a summary of the details of what you want from your career). Again, it is imperative that you identify what you want *before* you start your job search. Lack of focus is a main reason why most people take months to get hired and why most people end up in jobs they don't like. To develop your Dream Job Description, there are six key areas to consider:

1. Your ideal work location

2. Your ideal work schedule

3. Your ideal work environment/culture

4. Your ideal job function

5. Your ideal salary/compensation

6. Your ideal employer size

Several questions are provided for each area. As with the "big picture" questions, there are no right or wrong answers, and some questions will resonate with you more than others. By thinking through these questions, you will find it much easier to identify and evaluate job opportunities during your search.

There is one very important caveat before you begin this exercise: Be aware that these questions are just designed to help you focus and evaluate employers and positions. These questions should *not* be used to create a strict checklist.

### Your Ideal Work Location

► *Would you rather work in a major city, in the suburbs, or in a rural setting?*

► *How close to home do you want/need your work location to be?*

► *Are you willing to relocate from your current location? If so, how far from where you are now?*

## Your Ideal Work Schedule

► *Do you want a 9 to 5 job with a standard routine, or do you want to have a work schedule with more variety?*

► *How much travel do you want to do for work (and are you willing to do)?*

► *How many hours do you want to work per week (and are you willing to work per week)?*

## Your Ideal Work Environment/Culture

► *Do you want to work in an environment that is quiet and predictable (e.g., a library), in an environment that is loud and unpredictable (e.g., a Wall Street trading floor), or somewhere in between?*

► *Do you want to work in an environment that feels very corporate (i.e., you would have to wear a suit to work) or one that is more laid-back (i.e., you could wear jeans or exercise apparel to work)?*

► *Do you want to work in an environment that is very competitive or one that is very team-oriented?*

► *Do you want to work in an environment where employees socialize in and out of the office or one where people keep to themselves in and out of work?*

► *How much time do you want/need to spend outdoors vs. indoors?*

## Your Ideal Job Function

► *Which skills do you want to use on a daily basis?* Rank the following skill sets from 1 to 6, in terms of which you want to use most (a "1") and least (a "6"):

· Analytical/problem-solving skills
· Creativity skills
· Computer/technology skills
· Financial/organizational skills
· Interpersonal/communication skills
· Physical skills (e.g., building, repairing)

► *What knowledge/expertise do you want to use and develop even further?*

► *What results/impact do you want to achieve through your work?*

► *Do you prefer to work in isolation, or do you want to interact with other people for most of the day?*

► *Do you want to be managed very closely, or do you want more freedom on how to do your job?*

## Your Ideal Salary/Compensation

► *What types of income/compensation requirements do you have, and how important is salary to you?*

► *How important is it that your compensation be tied to your performance?* To research typical salary ranges for different fields for someone of your background, you can check out an online salary calculator. Salary websites have their limitations, but they can give you a range of what to expect. My favorite is the free salary calculator offered by the National Association of Colleges and Employers (NACE) at http://www.jobsearchintelligence.com. You can also get additional salary information by talking to people in various industries or job functions, although this is a delicate topic that many people are not comfortable discussing. If you are going to ask someone about salary, ask what someone in your position could expect to make initially and in the future. Do not ask someone how much money he is making.

## Your Ideal Employer Size

► *Do you want to work for a smaller employer (i.e., less than 100 employees) or a larger employer (i.e., 100–10,000 employees, or more)?* Size matters. Working for an employer with 27 total employees will be a very different experience from working for an employer with 27,000 total employees, so let's discuss key differences. It's similar to attending a major state school with 50,000 students vs. a small liberal arts college with fewer than 1,000 students. As a result, spend some time reflecting on what you liked or disliked about your collegiate environment. Here are four benefits (in general) of working for small organizations (fewer than 100 employees) and four benefits (in general) of working for larger organizations (100–10,000 employees, or more).

### Benefits of Working for Small Employers

1. *Greater individual impact.* Smaller employers often give new employees more responsibility at the start, simply because they have fewer people on staff. This can be rewarding since you can wear a lot of different hats, run your own projects, and even start projects of your own, all of which make it very easy for you and others to see the impact of your work.

2. *More day-to-day variety.* In many cases, your day-to-day

responsibilities can be much more diverse in a smaller organization. Many smaller employers also give their employees more freedom to determine how to get their work done.

3. *More intimacy with colleagues.* Because there are fewer employees, it's more likely you will get "face-time" with key executives and that you will get to know most of your colleagues.

4. *Faster growth potential.* Smaller employers usually have less bureaucracy and less complicated organizational structures. As a result, you can usually move up faster in a small organization. Large organizations usually have much more deliberate (i.e., slow) processes of promoting from within.

## Benefits of Working for Large Employers

1. *Greater organizational impact.* While your personal contribution might feel more significant in a small organization, the impact that your employer can have on the world is usually much more significant in a large organization, simply because of a much greater supply of resources (e.g., more employees, more financing, more equipment).

2. *More name recognition.* Working for a large organization that is a household name provides some advantages. First, you get to align yourself with the organization's brand the next time you look for a job. (Sorry, this will probably not be the last time you look for a job!) Second, small employers usually don't have as much name recognition within an industry.

3. *Greater stability.* Larger organizations are usually much more well established and stable than smaller organizations, which tend to have less predictable futures. However, anyone who worked at Circuit City or Lehman Brothers knows that this is not always true.

4. *More opportunities to change directions.* Larger employers

often have offices worldwide and are actually multiple organizations (sometimes in totally different markets) operating under one large umbrella. As a result, once you get inside a huge organization, there can be many more opportunities to move to new cities, branch out, and change professional directions. On the other hand, smaller employers often have fewer office locations (sometimes just one), and they often play in a very specific niche.

These are all broad generalizations that are definitely not true across the board. While you could likely achieve great success and satisfaction at a small or large employer (if you are in the right industry/position and working for a great organization), it's worth taking some time to think through your ideal company size. Most students and young professionals ignore small employers altogether, simply because they don't know what's out there.

Don't limit your job search to just organizations recruiting on your campus or organizations you are aware of through traditional advertising. In many ways, it is actually much easier to break into a smaller organization. It's considerably easier to connect with the real hiring decision-makers at small employers, and those individuals can usually move on hiring decisions much more quickly.

## IDENTIFY YOUR TARGET MARKET

After looking at the big picture and creating your Dream Job Description, your next step is to identify your Target Market. This will be a list of 10 to 20 ideal employers that meet the criteria you identified through the prior exercises and questions in this chapter. Most people would probably tell you that number is too small because most people aim way too low. All I will say in response is that this is a book on how to get your *dream job*. I'll also add that most of the people featured in this book targeted 10 to 20 employers (or fewer) during their job searches. Was it a coincidence that they succeeded with a focused strategy similar to the one I describe here?

Ideally, you want to create a target list of employers from *one* industry in *one* geographical region or city. If you want to broaden your search, do so carefully. As you add multiple industries and multiple regions to the mix, you lose focus. You also make it harder for people to help you.

There are a variety of ways you can research employers. However, I believe the most thorough, least expensive, and fastest way to generate your Target Market list is through www.Jigsaw.com, the world's largest database of updated, downloadable information on companies and their employees. The website is free to use (although there are premium membership options), and the directory features full contact information for millions of professionals, including job titles, company names, websites, mailing addresses, email addresses, and phone numbers. In just a few minutes, you can create a free account, and you can run searches to identify your Target Market of employers meeting your criteria for geography, industry, sub-industry, and so on. Just start somewhere. You can always broaden or refine your search later.

Jigsaw.com is a great tool, but it has some limitations, so I would encourage you to check out the following employer research resources as well:

► The world's #1 professional networking website: www.LinkedIn.com

► The Fortune 500 list

► The Inc. 5000 list

► For nonprofit research: www2.Guidestar.org

► Directories for Chambers of Commerce (which usually include lots of small businesses): www.uschamber.com.

You can also purchase employer lists through www.bizjournals.com and through association directories and membership lists.

You can also do employer research by checking out leading websites for your industry of choice. To be clear, I am *not* suggesting that you rely on job boards for employer research. I'm referring to websites (i.e., blogs or discussion boards) that cover trends and best-practices on your ideal industry.

## SHOULD I HAVE A BACKUP PLAN?

The quick answer to this question is *no*. Many people fail to get their dream job *because* they have a backup plan. Think about this logically. By having a backup plan, you are telling yourself that you might not succeed, which is exactly what you should *not* be thinking.

Before I start to get letters from pessimistic parents or career counselors saying that this is bad advice to give students and young professionals "in this economy," let me make sure you understand my message. I am not saying that you should target one organization and remain unemployed if you don't get hired by that employer. Having *any job* is better than being unemployed, given the stigma of being out of work.

What I am encouraging you to do is to commit to getting your dream job (i.e., getting hired by an employer from your Target Market ), no matter what it takes. Sure, in the meantime, you may have to stay in a job you don't love, or you may have to get a temporary job to pay the bills. However, you must commit 100 percent that you are going to get your dream job eventually. No excuses. No doubt. It is going to happen. It's only a matter of when, not if. It is that mindset that will actually help it happen because you will be more resilient and persistent.

> **LEIBMAN LIFE LESSON:**
> *A backup plan is actually a plan for failure. When you are willing to do whatever it takes, you will eventually get your dream job.*

If you knew you would die a slow, painful death if you did not get your dream job in the next six months, you would find a way to get that job. You would do absolutely whatever it took to get hired. Why not approach your dreams with the same vigor?

That probably sounds crazy, but most people completely miss the point of life and work. Don't just plug along in some job that you hate. Go after your dreams with everything you have! Hold absolutely nothing back, and you will succeed.

## Elissa Martins Got Her Dream Job with the Eastern District of Virginia

When I entered college, I had several ideas about what I wanted to do for a career. My journey took me through a variety of college and graduate courses and internships and jobs ranging from working at a psychiatric hospital to a research think tank, a law firm, a public defender's office, the Drug Enforcement Administration, the U.S. Probation Office for the District of Columbia, and more. Through these experiences, I learned what my passion was and which field was the best fit for me, ultimately finding my dream job in the field of probation.

When I first learned of the opening at the U.S. Probation Office for the Eastern District of Virginia, I was employed as a juvenile probation officer for the state of Virginia. At that time, I had only two years of experience working as a probation officer, but I took the chance and applied for the position with the federal government. To my surprise and happiness, I was called for an interview. I believe the core thing that differentiated me from the competition was my true love and passion for this profession. A career in the field of probation is not a job that you pursue for the money; it's a job you pursue because of your desire to help others reintegrate successfully into the community and make positive changes in their lives. I believe I was able to portray my dedication to the mission of probation, and when combined with my education and experience, this led to my being offered the position.

The best advice I would give to others on how to get their dream jobs after college would be to do what you love, not just what will pay the bills. It's funny to think that working with convicted felons is a dream job for me, but I love it and wouldn't change it for the world. No matter what your dream job is, go for it!

I got my dream job and so can you!

—ELISSA MARTINS

# CHAPTER 4

# MAKEOVER

## (STEP #3)

> "Nothing succeeds like the appearance of success."
> —CHRISTOPHER LASCH, U.S. HISTORIAN AND SOCIAL CRITIC

## $40 FOR A BOTTLE OF WATER?

Looks matter. If someone tells you that looks don't matter, he is wrong.

You don't need to look like Brad Pitt or Beyoncé to get your dream job and achieve career success, but you do have to put your best foot forward at all times. You tell the world what to think of you based on how you present yourself. Your family and closest friends may look past your appearance. However, employers and individuals you meet throughout your job search will subconsciously and instantaneously make judgments about your character, your personality, your intelligence, and your overall value as a human being based on what they see when they look at you. It might not be fair, but it's a reality.

You might not be comfortable with the analogy, but you need to see yourself as a product that you are marketing and selling. Looking your best is not about being phony or artificial. It's just about taking pride in your appearance and showing employers that if they hire you, you would represent them well.

You need to understand the concerns and negative stereotypes that employers and hiring persons have of students and young professionals. As discussed in Chapter 1, employers are concerned that you might be dishonest, lazy, difficult, uncommitted, unprofessional, and/or unqualified. Therefore, the first job of all of your self-marketing efforts is to eliminate these concerns. Then, your marketing needs to show employers that you believe in yourself and their organization, that you bring excellence to everything you do, that you have great people/communication skills, and that you can deliver the right results.

All of the Marketing Assets covered in this chapter need to leave employers thinking: "This person is exactly what we need. This person was destined to work for us. We absolutely must hire this person."

> LEIBMAN LIFE LESSON:
> Salary negotiations begin the moment you come in contact with a potential employer (long before you receive a job offer).

It is amazingly easy to stand out when you start your career because most young professionals have no idea how to present themselves to employers. Unfortunately, most job-seekers limit their earning potential and sabotage their chances of getting their dream job because they fail to look their best in person, on paper, and online. Is it possible to get your dream job without looking your best? Sure, anything is possible. But why make this process much harder than it needs to be?

Here's a quick example to demonstrate the power of appearances and marketing. A typical bottle of water sells for $1 or so at the store. However, there is a "luxury" brand of water endorsed by Jamie Foxx and other celebrities. It's called Bling H2O, and it has crystals embedded into the outside of each frosted-glass bottle. What does Bling H2O sell for? $40 per bottle! I've never drunk Bling H2O, but I'm willing to bet that it does not taste 40 times better than Poland Spring or Aquafina.

People pay more for products that *appear* to be of higher quality. Similarly, employers pay more for job candidates who appear to be of higher quality.

## 10 MARKETING ASSETS YOU NEED TO GET YOUR DREAM JOB

Do you want to feel better about yourself and have more confidence throughout your job search? Do you want to get your dream job faster? Do you want to make the interview process easier? Do you want to be offered a higher starting salary and a better compensation package? Then make sure you look your absolute best in person, on paper, and online before your job search even begins.

Your résumé is not your only marketing tool. This chapter will teach you 10 innovative Marketing Assets that will make you look like you are worth a million bucks:

**1.** Confident Body Language

**2.** Polished Physical Appearance

**3.** Rock-Solid References

**4.** Results-Oriented Résumé

**5.** Compelling Cover Letter

**6.** Pristine Internet Presence

**7.** Pumped-Up LinkedIn Profile

**8.** Strategic Social Media Account

**9.** Email/Voicemail Marketing Machine

**10.** Winner's Mindset

## Marketing Asset #1: Confident Body Language

It takes less than three seconds to blow your chances of getting your dream job. Yes, you can actually lose the interview (or your chances of getting a referral) within three seconds of meeting someone.

What you say is often not nearly as important as *how* you say it. Most students and young professionals *underestimate* the importance of making a positive first impression, while they *overestimate* their present ability to do so.

When you meet someone for the first time in any setting, your initial goal should be to appear trustworthy, likable, confident, and professional. Don't be intimidated by this objective, which is actually really easy to achieve if you follow these five body language secrets:

1. *Smile first and often.* Yes, this sounds incredibly obvious, but most people don't smile nearly enough. A genuine smile is inviting and contagious. Always be the first person to smile. If someone is not smiling at you, it's usually because you are not smiling at her. A genuine smile conveys friendliness, removes barriers, and encourages others to want to get to know you. A warm smile immediately makes you more likable.

2. *Give a strong (not suffocating) handshake.* A strong handshake conveys confidence and integrity, while a weak handshake makes you look like someone without any backbone. Having said that, do not try to devour the other person's hand. Just make a nice, firm shake with two to three pumps up and down.

3. *Maintain consistent (not creepy) eye contact.* Eye contact also indicates confidence, trust, and interest in the other person, which further makes you more likable. While shaking hands and smiling at someone, look him right in the eye. Then, be sure to maintain eye contact for the majority of the conversation. (Warning: Like a bone-crushing handshake, eye contact can also be taken too far.)

4. *Stand up, sit up.* You shouldn't try to look like a statue, but standing up straight (or sitting up straight) makes you look more confident.

5. *Remove meaningless movements.* Fidgeting, tapping your foot, covering your face with your hands or fingers, and other purposeless, nervous body language make you look unconfident and make the people around you feel awkward. If you feel uncomfortable and need to release some energy through your body, just focus on moving your toes around inside your shoe (without tapping your foot).

## Marketing Asset #2: Polished Physical Appearance

If you want people to respect you as a job-seeker (and as an employee), you must also dress in a manner that screams, "I am a professional!" Any chance of a job offer (or promotion) can be eliminated if you don't look the part, no matter how talented you are.

Clothing can make you look taller and thinner or shorter and fatter. More important, clothing can transform the way others see you as well as the way you feel about yourself. I asked Kim Foley, president of Professional Image Strategies, for some help in designing a concise summary of how to dress for success in the workplace. For more than 25 years, as a professional stylist and makeup artist for film and television, Kim has worked with presidents, heads of state, leaders in industry, political candidates, celebrities, and many other high-profile individuals.

In general, Kim suggests that you keep it simple and not try to make fashion statements. Dressing for a date or a social event with friends is very different from dressing for the workplace. Your #1 goal should be to dress for credibility. Here are seven more specific rules to make sure you dress for success in any professional setting:

1. *Dress for the environment.* Looking "professional" can unfortunately mean something different based on the specific

employer or event. In general, corporate America expects you to dress in a manner that is understated, classic, and conservative. Wear a business suit for any professional event or for any sort of interview. Do not use TV shows, celebrities, or pop-culture advertisements as a guide for how you should dress in the workplace. If you are ever unsure of what to wear, just ask what is appropriate, and err on the side of being overdressed. Keep in mind that certain work environments may also look down upon unique hairstyles, visible tattoos, body piercings, and so on. This might sound superficial and unfair, but it's a reality.

2.  *Pay attention to details.* You must match from head to toe. Also, avoid any funky patterns. For men, Kim says that shoes and belt must be the same color, socks must match your pants, and your tie should end a half-inch below the top of your belt when you are standing up straight. For women, Kim says that stockings should not have any patterns or colors, and they should always match your skin tone. She also says that women should remove any chipped nail polish and wear a neutral nail color, if any.

3.  *Fit matters more than brand.* You don't need to spend thousands of dollars on the most expensive clothing lines, but you do need to make sure your clothes fit correctly for your body. You have probably already been told not to wear anything that is too tight or shows too much skin (Kim says women should never wear anything that shows "even a hint of cleavage"), but you should also not wear clothes that are too loose. Clothes that are very baggy make you look sloppy and like a little kid. Kim also says that hems of pants should never touch the ground, and sleeve length for shirts and jackets should be customized for your arm length. You can visit your local dry cleaner or tailor for help with alterations.

4.  *Shoes or lose.* Always wear a nice pair of shoes, and make sure they are not worn out and that they are clean and nicely pol-

ished. For men, Kim says not to wear shoes that have thick soles that look like tire treads. Kim says that no matter how "dressy," flip flops are only acceptable in extremely casual workplaces. She adds that strappy shoes or stiletto heels are not acceptable.

5. *Keep it crisp and fresh.* Make sure your clothes are nicely ironed, not worn out or outdated, and free of any holes or stains. (Check your clothes in a well-lit area where stains can be seen.) Kim says she has plenty of stories of job-seekers who tried their clothes on the night before (or day of) a big interview, only to learn that their clothes no longer fit or had a hole or stain. At that point, it is often too late to find a suitable replacement. As a result, she recommends checking your wardrobe a week in advance of any professional event to allow time for tailoring or cleaning if necessary.

6. *Smell swell and be clean.* This sounds obvious, but it is worth repeating. If you have any offensive odor emanating from your body, you have absolutely no chance of getting hired. Shower, brush your teeth, and wear deodorant before entering any professional situation. Kim says to save colognes or perfumes for social situations, and make sure you are nicely groomed from head to toe.

7. *Accessorize appropriately.* A sharp tie, a nice watch, or a tasteful piece of jewelry can be a great finishing touch to an outfit, but don't go overboard. Kim says that men should avoid jewelry in conservative workplaces, and women should stay away from trendy shoes and jewelry and wear more sophisticated, classic, understated items. Remember: The goal isn't to look hip. The goal is to look credible.

You can also visit www.KimFoley.com for additional tips or to schedule a personal or Skype consultation with Kim.

## Marketing Asset #3: Rock-Solid References

A common question from the audience when I speak to groups about how to get your dream job is: "How do I sell myself without bragging?"

Here is my best answer: *Get the right people to brag for you.*

A strategic testimonial from the right person is your most powerful marketing asset. In short, if someone else says you are great, a hiring person will often assume you are as well. As a result, endorsements can increase your chances of getting an interview, and they can also make the interview process easier. However, all testimonials are not created equal. Here are seven little-known secrets for using endorsements to get your dream job:

1. *Get endorsed by people who love you.* Sounds obvious, right? Well, I haven't always done this, and you probably haven't either. When I was in high school, my family learned from one of the colleges that rejected me that one of my letters of recommendation had been a factor in my rejection. (Don't ask me how my Dad figured this out!) Apparently, my history teacher wrote a paltry, cookie-cutter letter on my behalf. We were surprised at this, but I should have known better. I had asked him for a letter because I had thought he was a brilliant writer, but he had not been one of my biggest advocates. Big mistake.

2. *Get endorsed by people who are reliable.* I once asked a former boss to serve as a reference. This guy was a big fan of mine, so I figured he'd be perfect. However, the letter he gave me to submit had several typos and did not even include a standard header. It looked terrible. Luckily, I saw the letter before it went out. I should not have been surprised. He was a great guy but one of the most disorganized people I knew. Make sure your references have their act together. If they aren't normally reliable and thorough, they won't suddenly become reliable and thorough when communicating with people on your behalf. If your references look bad, you will look bad. The opposite is also true.

3. *Get endorsed by people who "look like" those you want to impress.* For example, if you are applying for a financial services job where you would report to a director of finance, it would be much more impressive to have a recommendation from your corporate finance professor than your history professor. This is not always possible, so do what you can.

4. *Tell your references how to endorse you.* This might sound sneaky or conniving, but most people have no idea what to write or say in a testimonial or letter of recommendation. As a result, most testimonials are the worthless, generic kind, like "Pete is a great guy. I highly recommend him." Here's a confession for you. Many of the best testimonials I have ever gotten are endorsements I have written myself and gotten permission to attribute to another person. Many people actually thank me for making it easier for them to endorse me. Use your judgment on this one. Some people are more comfortable with this than others, and you can't ask for this unless someone has seen the quality of your work and the two of you have a very strong relationship.

5. *Tell your references what to say if asked about your weaknesses.* In 2010, one of my former colleagues asked me to serve as a reference for him. Given the work that I do and being very thorough, I thought about how to respond if a hiring person asked me what this person's greatest weakness was. Can you guess what the *first* question was when his future boss called me? Luckily, I had a well-constructed comeback planned, which I conveniently sandwiched between a discussion of the person's strengths. The chances of your references thinking about this in advance are close to zero. It's your responsibility to prep them on what to say if asked about your deficiencies. If you don't, they might step on a landmine for you.

6. *Create a Recommendation Report.* With a Recommendation Report, you cut out the fluff found in most letters of recommendation where the writers talk about their background and

how they know you. This is a tool where you get former colleagues, bosses, customers, professors, etc. to provide (or approve) one- to three-sentence testimonials about you and your work. Then, you list each person's name, title/affiliation, and results-oriented quotes. Contact information can also be included for each reference. Consider the value of having three to five quotes like the following on a one-page document that you could include when you apply for a job:

> *"Reliable, enthusiastic, professional, and a terrific communicator. . . . Katie Johnson would be an extremely valuable asset to any organization."*

> *"Katie Johnson's track record as a marketer speaks for itself. She has the experience, knowledge, and innate personality traits to make any project highly profitable."*

7. *Post your endorsements online.* Wouldn't it be cool to have your own TV channel for your job search where you could feature other people talking about how amazing you are? Well, thanks to YouTube, this is now possible. Yes, YouTube is not just for videos of dancing birds, talking dogs, or celebrity bloopers.

Go to www.youtube.com and create your very own TV channel at www.youtube.com/yourname. (This is much easier to do than it sounds.) You can use a flip camera or your cell phone to film several 30- to 60-second testimonials from current/former bosses, colleagues, customers, or professors. Then, upload them to your channel. An enthusiastic video testimonial is much more compelling than a text testimonial because it includes body language and tone. You can also take these video testimonials and insert them into your email signature and other social media profiles (e.g., your LinkedIn profile, your Facebook account). While not everyone will be comfortable with

> LEIBMAN LIFE LESSON:
> *The best way to brag is to get the right people to brag for you.*

appearing on video, it's definitely worth asking your best advocates.

## Marketing Asset #4: Results-Oriented Résumé

I still remember the look of horror on my professor's face when I showed her my first résumé when I was a student in college. Being proud of my GPA, I had used a huge, funky font to draw attention to it. Somehow thinking that this would not make it obvious enough, I also bolded it and put it in italics. Unfortunately, that was just one of the many résumé errors I made. Luckily, I was not too proud to ask for help.

You might not have souped-up your résumé like I did, but your current résumé probably needs a lot of work as well. I've reviewed résumés from some of the world's most talented students and from some extremely successful young professionals and senior executives, and I'm convinced that most résumés are very damaging to the job-seeker's perceived value.

In general, job-seekers make two huge mistakes with résumés. First, most résumés have very poor formatting. Second, most résumés have very poor content. Before we discuss how you can write a Results-Oriented Résumé, let's go over six little-known résumé secrets.

1. *At best, résumés are skimmed (not read).* A hiring person will not spend more than 10 to 15 seconds reading your résumé, if she takes the time to read it at all.

2. *Your résumé must be 100 percent flawless.* Even though your résumé will just be glanced at, it takes only one typo for it to get thrown in the trash. This might sound harsh, but think about it from an employer's perspective. If you cannot produce a one-page document that is error-free, how could you be trusted to handle a more significant project?

3. *Résumés are used as a screening tool.* When employers read your résumé, they are looking for a reason to remove you

from consideration, not for a reason to bring you in for an interview.

4. *Your résumé should not focus on responsibilities.* Employers care about your prior *results* because past performance is a predictor of future performance. In other words, what you have done is not nearly as important as *what happened* because of what you have done. Most résumés are not compelling because they focus on responsibilities, rather than results.

5. *Employers don't hire résumés. Employers hire people.* I cringe when reading job search books that focus 25 percent or more of their pages on résumés. If I had to assign a percentage to the role a résumé plays in a job search, I would estimate less than 10 percent, because of the importance of attitude, body language, networking and interviewing skills, and so on. As mentioned above, a bad résumé can certainly remove you from consideration. Your résumé is important, but its value is very limited. The most a résumé can do is keep you in the mix.

6. *There are no official résumé rules.* There is no official template your résumé must follow and no absolute rule for writing a résumé. As a result, you should design your résumé in a way that makes you look your best. Every single line in your résumé should help your cause and be worded in the most impressive fashion possible, *without lying*. For example, if your major is 100 percent irrelevant to the job you are applying for, feel free to leave your major off your résumé. If your GPA within your major is 3.6 and your cumulative GPA is 3.2, list just your GPA within your major. If your GPA is under 3.0, then don't include it. You can also be creative (within reason) with your prior job titles. For example, my title during my last three years with the Washington Wizards was "Manager, Group Sales." However, if I was applying for another sales job now, the title on my résumé would include one of my achievements and read "Manager, Group Sales, and 3-time #1 NBA Salesperson of the Year," since that was one of

my awards during my tenure with the franchise. Since people just glance at résumés, consider including achievements in your titles, and feel free to repeat your achievements throughout the résumé. Bottom line: Play by your own rules. Just be 100 percent honest and stay within reason.

Writing a Results-Oriented Résumé is easy if you break it down into the following six phases. This process will help you understand what you have to offer and what you can discuss during interviews.

## Phase 1: Brainstorm

Start by writing down everything that could have any relevance to your job search, and make sure not to focus only on the obvious (i.e., academic and professional experience). You won't ultimately use everything in the final version of your résumé, but you have to start somewhere. Employers want well-rounded employees; unique experiences can also help you stand out in a good way. Don't worry if you don't have anything to write down for some of the categories below:

► Educational background, including college(s) attended, courses studied, GPA, major/minor, academic honors, academic affiliations (e.g., fraternities, sororities, honor societies)

► Personal or professional activities, affiliations, and memberships

► Leadership positions/experience

► Work experience (i.e., part-time jobs, full-time jobs, internships)

► Military experience

► Athletic experience

► Volunteer/service experience

- International/travel experience

- "Hard" skills (e.g., computer/Internet skills)

- "Soft" skills (e.g., communication skills)

- Interests

- Certifications

- Honors and awards

- Presentations delivered

- Articles published

- Other languages spoken

- Intellectual property (e.g., patents, copyrights, trademarks)

**Phase 2: Build**

The next phase is to start building your actual résumé. In general, there are five major sections, as outlined below:

1. *Contact information.* This should be at the top of your résumé and should include your full name, mailing address, email address, and phone number. You can also include links to your social media profiles if they will help your case. Make sure to use professional contact information, such as KimDavidson@gmail.com for your email address. Something like sexyterpschick234@gmail.com is not acceptable.

2. *Summary.* This could be a one- to two-sentence paragraph or a bulleted list of key achievements or career highlights. This is different from a meaningless "Objective," which usually has no value for you or the employer (e.g., "Seeking entry-level position where I can utilize my superior communication skills").

3. *Experience.* This can include leadership experience, work experience, and volunteer/service experience. Your experience can be broken out in multiple sections or combined into one section entitled "Experience."

4. *Education.* You can include your major, year you graduated (or expected graduation date), GPA within major or cumulative GPA (use whichever is higher and leave it out if less than 3.0), any academic honors, and even a brief description of the college you attended (e.g., "Ranked as the #17 college in the world by *U.S. News & World Report*"). In general, you usually want to keep the "Education" section below the "Experience" section on your résumé because you look less experienced if you put the "Education" section at the top of your résumé. However, this depends on your individual situation.

5. *Extras.* This can include relevant activities, skills, interests, and so on. You can break them into different sections or lump them together into an "Activities and Skills" section.

Last point: Do not include a line that says "References available upon request." It's like writing "Willing to meet with you for an interview."

## Phase 3: Quantify

Do not assume anything is obvious when writing your résumé. Use numbers as much as possible to quantify your achievements and performance. For example, when I was in college, I was inducted into the Phi Beta Kappa Society. PBK is a very prestigious honor society, so I assumed people would know what it was. However, a résumé writer suggested that I quantify what it meant to be accepted into that organization. Here is how I referred to this honor before and after her suggestion. Which looks better?

► Before: *Inducted into the Phi Beta Kappa Society upon graduation from JHU.*

► After: *Awarded Phi Beta Kappa Society Membership, which recognizes only 1% of top college students nationwide each year.*

Your résumé must also focus on quantifiable *results*, not on responsibilities. Here is another change I made to my résumé back in 2008 while looking for a new job. Which looks better?

► Before: *Managed 7 different sales representatives between 2006 and 2008.*

► After: *Managed 7 different sales representatives to the highest sales numbers of each of their careers.*

**Phase 4: Format**

After quantifying your achievements, you need to format your résumé and make it easy to read. Here are some best-practices for formatting:

► *Tighten it up.* Some 99 percent of students (and most young professionals) should keep their résumé to one page. Your résumé should not include everything you brainstormed in Phase 1; the résumé should focus on just what is most relevant in selling yourself to your ideal employers. I occasionally see two- to three-page résumés from students who have never even had a full-time job. In order to tighten up your résumé, you should remove any unnecessary words and avoid situations where one of your bulleted statements has only one to two words that run over to the next line. If you use bullets appropriately and play around with margins and fonts, you can get a lot of text on one page, while still leaving room for white space.

► *Be consistent and write correctly.* Develop a clean, consistent look throughout your résumé. Each job/position should be formatted exactly the same way in regard to font type, font size, spacing, caps, etc. Use a professional font (e.g., Times New Roman, size 11) and use italics and bolding cautiously. "I" should not appear anywhere on your résumé, nor should you write in full sentences. You must also use the correct tense based on whether the tasks/achievements you include are ongoing or finished.

If you are a student struggling to fill up one page, you can include relevant coursework and relevant personal interests. You can also include a one- to two-sentence description of any of your prior employers, which can be beneficial even if you don't need to fill up space.

## Phase 5: Refine

Proofread, proofread, proofread. You should also get several of your friends, professors, and/or professional contacts to look at your résumé, and tell them they have only 10 to 15 seconds to look at it and to give you their impressions. Then, after they give you their initial feedback, they can analyze your résumé line-by-line for additional suggestions. Another idea is to offer a friend $10 for each typo she finds in your résumé. Better to lose $20 to a friend than to lose thousands of dollars and miss out on getting your dream job by having two typos in the résumé you submit.

## Phase 6: Customize

Phases 1 to 5 in writing your résumé will leave you with a great template to share with your contacts during your job search. However, when you apply for an actual position, you should personalize each résumé based on the job description. If no job description is provided, just design your résumé based on what you find on the employer's website. As your career progresses and you develop more experience and honors, you will find that your résumé could look very different based on the job you are applying for.

## Marketing Asset #5: Compelling Cover Letter

Always include a Compelling Cover Letter, even if it's not requested by an employer. A well-written letter is a powerful marketing tool that can bring your résumé to life. It can help you stand out by demonstrating your passion, your personality, and your strong written communication skills. Upon reading your cover letter, you want the hiring person to think, "Wow, this person is exactly what we need. This person was destined to work here." Every single line of your cover letter must serve a purpose and demonstrate your value to the employer. While there is no official template that your cover letter must abide by, here are four secrets for writing a cover letter that will significantly increase your chances of getting an interview.

1. *Take pride in the appearance of the letter.* Like your résumé, your cover letter must be error-free (no typos or run-on sentences) and structured professionally.

2. *Personalize the letter based on the job.* If no job description is provided, refer to the employer's website for ideas. The letter should be addressed to a specific person (not "to whom it may concern"), and you should reference the position you want. Explain how you have made other people or organizations better in a way that is relevant to the job you are applying for. While being concise (keep your letter to one page), use specific examples or stories to show how you have the skills and traits needed for success in the position. Your letter should demonstrate why you want the job *and* why the employer should want to hire you.

3. *Build your credibility through shared connections or affiliations.* For example, if you were referred to the hiring person, you should definitely mention that at the beginning of your letter. If not, try to find a connection within the organization that you can reference or some other shared connection or affiliation. If nothing else, you can include a relevant one- to two-sentence endorsement (as a quote) from one of your academic or professional contacts.

4. *Close with a call-to-action.* Do not leave your follow-up in the hands of the hiring person. End your letter with something like, "I will call you next week to answer any questions you may have and to discuss how I can help _____ [insert

employer name] achieve _____ [insert the specific results the employer mentioned in the job description]. You may also reach me at xxx-xxx-xxxx or firstname.lastname@gmail.com in the meantime."

## Marketing Asset #6: Pristine Internet Presence

Have you "Googled" yourself lately? If not, why not?

If an employer is thinking about investing thousands of dollars by hiring you, you better believe the hiring people will do everything in their power to check you out online. This starts by typing your full name into www.google.com to see what comes back.

Go to www.google.com right now and type your name (in quotations) into its search feature and see what comes up on the first page. You might find that you do not seem to exist on the Internet (i.e., nothing comes up for your name, or you are buried behind other people with the same name)—or you might not like what you find.

I did a Google search on my name in 2010 and found a link to a website where another person named Pete Leibman had a short message about his desire to "take over the world." I'm sure the guy was kidding around, but it sounded a little creepy. More important, I didn't want people to know that was my intention for the year 2020. (Just kidding . . . sorry, I couldn't resist. . . .)

So, I looked the guy up on LinkedIn, emailed him, complimented him on his awesome name (get it?), and politely asked him to remove the message. He thanked me for the email, said he did not even realize the message was online, and immediately took it down. Problem solved.

The first step in controlling your online identity is to try to remove anything negative you find about yourself online. Most of the time, when you find something damaging, it will either be something you posted yourself or something posted by someone you know. In either case, it can often be removed without much effort. After you clean up anything negative, you should also make sure employers will see some positive information when they search for you online. Most people are not this proactive, so this gives you yet another way to stand out. This is where the power of the Internet and social media can work in a job-seeker's favor.

Do you own the website address for yourname.com? If not, put down this book, go back online, and buy it right now through godaddy.com or another source. At the minimum, this prevents someone else from setting up a website at yourname.com. You can also turn that domain name into a one-page personal website for yourself, although your LinkedIn profile can serve that purpose as well. (We'll discuss LinkedIn later in this chapter.) Last, if you ever plan to start your own business, you will definitely want to own the domain name for your name. In other words, it's definitely worth the small investment (about $10 per year).

If you have a name that is often misspelled, you should also consider buying the domain names for the common misspellings. This is not an issue if your last name is Smith. This is an issue if your last name is something like Wojciechowski.

You can also set up a "Google alert" for your name at www. google.com/alerts so that you receive automatic notifications any time something is published online mentioning your name.

## Give Your Facebook Page a Face-Lift

Back in 2005, my younger brother, Matt, was interviewing for a summer internship position with a small PR firm in Philadelphia. Midway through the interview, the hiring person looked at Matt and said, "Can you explain the following quote from your Facebook page to me? On your page, you wrote 'It's not that I'm lazy. It's that I just don't care.' What did you mean by that?" (In case you have not seen the movie *Office Space*, that quote is a line from Peter Gibbons, the lead character in the movie.) My brother is actually one of the hardest working people I know, and he was just trying to be funny. However, the person interviewing him was not laughing.

Here's the scariest part of that story. Matt's Facebook profile was set to "private" and the interviewer did not even have an account on Facebook, yet he got onto my brother's page anyway. (This was in 2005, when less than 5 million people were on the social networking website; as of 2011, more than *800 million* people use Facebook.) The interviewer was able to access my brother's account through an intern at the company who happened to be Facebook "friends" with Matt. Through the intern, the hiring person had access to every quote, comment, wall post, and picture on Matt's page. Yikes. . . .

Setting your Facebook page to "private" is a step in the right direction, but it's not enough. It amazes me what people post on their Facebook pages for the world to see. Here are the exact words from one of the craziest Facebook wall posts I have seen a person post on his page. Well, this is the craziest post from those that were considered "acceptable for print":

> *"What an FFFFFFinnnng night!!! It wouldn't be a bro night without everyone taking their shirts off at the club and eventually getting thrown out and pissing on the bouncer's car. Then Alpy raging in the streets!!!*

Would you hire someone who made a post like this on Facebook? Unless this person's dream job is to get cast on *Jersey Shore*, his chances of getting hired would be eliminated.

A 2009 study by Microsoft showed that more than 70 percent of hiring managers had rejected a job candidate based on what they found when looking the candidate up online. That number has surely increased by now and will only go up in the future. You can still have fun online, but you need to be smart about how you portray yourself to the world. Here are four best-practices for managing your account on Facebook or any other social media site:

1.  *Remove anything questionable from your account.* It takes just one stupid picture, comment, or wall post (from you or a friend) to taint the image a prospective employer has of you.

2.  *Keep your privacy settings strict.* Employers are looking at your page only to see if there is a reason to disqualify you. Keep your entire page private to people who are not friends with you.

3.  *Use a respectable profile picture.* You don't have to be in a suit, but your picture should still represent you well. In other

words, it's not a great idea to use a profile picture of yourself from a recent "pimps and hos" costume party. (That might sound bad, but I have unfortunately seen much worse.) Even if you keep your privacy settings strict, your profile picture will usually be viewable to everyone searching for your name, so this is important.

4. *Assume that everything (pictures, videos, and text) on your page can be seen by everyone.* Just because your profile is set to private does not mean that employers still can't access your profile, like they did with my brother.

## Marketing Asset #7: Pumped-Up LinkedIn Profile

LinkedIn is the world's #1 professional networking website, with more than 120 million worldwide members (as of 2011). Leaders from every industry have a presence on the website (it is not just for the business world), and a new member joins the site every second of every day, on average. Despite these amazing statistics, many young job-seekers ignore this revolutionary tool. Of those who have accounts, few take the time to design profiles that represent them well.

When I first learned about LinkedIn in 2006 before the site really took off, I was very skeptical because I didn't understand it. However, after spending hundreds of hours studying its inner functionality and using it to advance my own career, I became a *big* believer.

In case you don't think it's worth the time to figure out how to use LinkedIn for your job search (a huge mistake), you need to understand that LinkedIn is a tool that can skyrocket your career *after* you get hired as well. The site is used every day by people worldwide to build new relationships, strengthen existing relationships, conduct research on industry best-practices, identify sales/networking leads, and generate revenue.

You will learn how to *use* LinkedIn as part of your job search strategy in Chapters 5 and 6. For now, let's just focus on designing your profile. LinkedIn expert Lewis Howes suggests that you think of your LinkedIn profile as "better than a résumé on steroids." I like his analogy.

Like the average résumé, most LinkedIn profiles also have *a lot* of room for improvement. A poorly designed LinkedIn profile can actually hurt your personal brand. On the other hand, a well-constructed LinkedIn profile can be one of your greatest marketing tools. For an example of a well-constructed LinkedIn profile, check mine out at www.LinkedIn.com/in/PeteLeibman.

Here are 10 ways to pump up your LinkedIn profile.

1. *Start at* learn.linkedin.com. This is a free resource from LinkedIn to help you get started. You can watch several short videos to set up your account. I'll focus next on what to do after you learn the basics there.

2. *Use a professional headshot.* Most people on LinkedIn ether have no headshot at all or they use a picture that is hard to see or unprofessional. Since LinkedIn is a professional networking website, your picture should be a headshot from the neck up, and you should be in professional attire. (You should not be wearing a baseball cap or a bicycle helmet, unless that's what you would be wearing to work in the job you want.) If you don't have a great headshot picture, just put on some business attire and get a friend to take a picture of you against a solid white wall.

3. *Maximize your headline.* Most LinkedIn profile headlines are boring, unoriginal, hard to understand, or simply damaging to your perceived value. Like a good "elevator pitch" (which we will cover in Chapter 6), your headline should be clear, original, and compelling. Your headline is valuable real estate, so don't waste any of the 120 characters LinkedIn gives you. Either list one or two relevant, impressive achievements or use a five- to 10-word description of how you could make other people/organizations better. If you have space in your headline, you can also include your email address so that you are easily accessible to anyone who wants to connect with you.

4. *Spice up your summary.* A great summary should be written to impress your target market of employers. It should include your contact information (your email address at the minimum), several relevant achievements, your dream or professional mission, and a story showing why you are passionate about your dream or professional mission. Stories are very powerful in a job search (more to come on that in Chapter 7). You can write your summary in the third person, or you can use bullets. Summaries written in the first person tend to sound arrogant when discussing achievements.

5. *Make sure your specialties are specific.* All of your specialties should fit within the image you want to give out. As your career progresses, you could have a wide variety of specialties. Only list specialties relevant to the career you want.

6. *Craft your current and past positions.* This includes your title and a description for each position. For the most part, you can simply copy-and-paste what you have used on your résumé. Again, feel free to be strategic with your titles (as discussed above in the "Results-Oriented Résumé" section). As with the "Experience" section of your résumé, you can also include volunteer and extracurricular activities here and leadership positions (not just work experience). However, as on your résumé, you should not list every single job/experience you have ever had. Just include those that are relevant and beneficial to your job search and career goals.

7. *Enhance your education.* Rather than just showing the schools you have attended, you can also cite one of your academic achievements in parentheses next to where you list your academic institution. (Again, you can check out my profile at www.LinkedIn.com/in/PeteLeibman to see how I do this.)

8. *Request recommendations.* Follow the tips from the "Rock-Solid References" section of this chapter and get at least three recommendations on your LinkedIn profile.

9. *Get to 100 percent.* Make sure your profile is professional and 100 percent complete and consistent with your paper résumé. While a typo on your LinkedIn profile is not as serious as a typo on your résumé, you should still design your LinkedIn profile with care.

10. *Get your vanity URL.* Use a "vanity" name for the web page for your LinkedIn profile (e.g., www.LinkedIn.com/in/PeteLeibman). Your vanity name is very search-friendly when people Google you. This is much easier to include in your email signature (hint) or at the top of your résumé (hint) than the traditional URL that LinkedIn gives you when you sign up for an account.

## Marketing Asset #8: Strategic Social Media Account

Social media sites provide unbelievable personal branding opportunities to job-seekers that were not available a few years ago. (This is one of the reasons why now is the best time ever to get your dream job.) The type of job you are looking for will dictate how to use other platforms in addition to LinkedIn and Facebook. Here are three ideas on how to leverage social media to be even more marketable to employers.

1. *Tweet.* Set up an account at www.Twitter.com and tweet your own tips (or links to tips/articles from other sources) related to your field.

2. *Blog.* Set up a blog at www.WordPress.com or any other blogging platform and write a weekly article (300–500 words each) to demonstrate your written communication skills, along with your expertise/passion for your field. You can also serve as a "guest blogger" on an existing blog (if you don't want to set up a blog of your own).

3. *Film.* Set up a TV channel at www.youtube.com and post tips in a weekly video (one to two minutes long) to demonstrate

your presentation and verbal communication skills, along with your expertise/passion for your field.

Again, your strategy here will depend on the type of job you want and what your strengths are. You can do one of the above, or you can brainstorm another way to increase your value through a social media platform. Very few job-seekers go to this effort, allowing you to stand out in a great way.

## Marketing Asset #9: Email/Voicemail Marketing Machine

Your email account is a marketing tool that most job-seekers take for granted. You will likely have a lot of email communications with potential employers and referral sources during your job search. Here are some tips to impress people with your email signature:

- ► Use your full name.

- ► Use a professional email address.

- ► Include your phone number.

- ► Include a relevant title/affiliation/achievement.

- ► Remove any inspirational quotes. (People don't want to read them.)

- ► Don't use any wacky fonts or background colors. (I've received emails I can barely read.)

- ► Include a link to your relevant social media accounts.

You should also make sure the voicemail greeting on your cell phone is friendly and professional. Just record a short, simple message like "Hi, you've reached Pete Leibman. Please leave a message and I'll get right back to you. Have a great day." Then, call your voicemail from another phone to make sure you sound good and to make sure there is no background noise or music. You might think it's cool to have Jay-Z or Katy Perry blasting in the background, but the average hiring person won't find it amusing.

## Marketing Asset #10: Winner's Mindset

The last component of a compelling personal brand is the one that is most often overlooked in job search books: your attitude and how you appear to yourself. Your mindset will ultimately be the #1 factor in determining whether or not you eventually get your dream job. A beautiful résumé and a stellar LinkedIn profile are worthless if you don't believe you are worthy of landing your dream job. Lack of belief will sabotage you in ways you will not even be aware of.

In Chapters 1 and 2, you learned the importance of being open-minded to possibility and being willing to start through faith. Initially, you don't need to *believe* you will succeed. You just need to start. However, you ultimately have to shift from open-mindedness that your dream is possible to confidence that your dream is inevitable.

There was no single moment when that transformation occurred for me during my quest in college. It happened somewhere along the way, as I built momentum through the actions you will learn about in Chapters 5 and 6. After starting my journey through faith, I encountered a lot of people who were not as optimistic as I was about my dream. I initially felt sorry for myself. However, my mindset quickly shifted to: *"You know what? I'm going to show them. These people don't have any idea what they are talking about. They are wrong. I am going to succeed."*

It's important to point out that there was no guarantee or visible proof that my beliefs were true. All that mattered was that my beliefs empowered me to *keep going*. Ultimately, my beliefs *became true* because I believed they were true.

When I interviewed with the Wizards the second time around (remember, I was rejected for an internship position as a junior in college), I went into the process believing to the bottom of my soul that I was destined to land that job. I honestly believed that the organization would have to be stupid *not* to hire me. I obviously did not tell the Wizards that, and I don't say this to impress you or to pretend that I was not nervous. Instead, I tell you what I was thinking to emphasize the importance of believing in yourself. Without confidence in myself, I would have quit my search too soon and I would not have gotten my dream job. Likewise, if you don't believe that you can get your dream job, an employer will not believe in you either, and you will probably quit too soon.

**When it comes to your dreams,
it is *always* too soon to give up.**

Belief in yourself will make you more resourceful because you will be more open to the opportunities around you, many of which you can't even see right now. Belief will also make you more resilient because you will know it's just a matter of when, not if.

In order to get your dream job, you eventually need to shift your thought process from "I'll try" to "This is absolutely going to happen. I am destined for this job." That might sound crazy for you to believe at this point. Be patient. Development of a solid belief system is unfortunately not something that happens instantaneously. In the meantime, use criticism or doubters to fuel your fire, and stay focused on your strengths. (In Chapter 8, you will also learn "The 10 Commandments for Concrete Confidence.")

> LEIBMAN LIFE LESSON:
> *You have to have a winner's mindset before you can become a winner.*

## LOOKS MATTER, BUT THEY ARE NOT "EVERYTHING"

In 2011, I attended a seminar by a "personal branding expert" who had business cards with a tagline that stated "Image is everything."

I hate to knock her catchy slogan, but she is wrong. While looks definitely matter, they are only one piece of the "puzzle." No one came and handed me or any of the other people in this book our dream jobs just because of how we looked. Nope, we all went out and got our dream jobs. Keep reading to learn how you can, too.

CHAPTER 5

# PLAN

## (STEP #4)

> "People who make the worst use of their time are the same ones who complain that there is never enough time."
>
> —ANONYMOUS

## DO YOU DRIP SWEAT WHEN YOU EXERCISE?

People do some bizarre things in the gym, and I'm not just talking about falling off treadmills. (Yes, I have seen that happen more than once.) I'm talking about approaching exercise sessions with a complete lack of focus and intensity. In one recent visit to the gym, I saw someone filling out a crossword puzzle while using a leg curl machine, I saw another person take nearly 10 minutes to read the newspaper between two sets of crunches, and I saw a pair of exercise buddies spend nearly 20 minutes chatting between two sets of lunges. Then, these people wonder why they aren't making any progress toward their fitness goals, even though they are "spending hours each week exercising."

I can do more good for my body in one hour at the gym than some people do in 20 hours. There are two reasons why. First, I know which exercises provide the most value. Second, I'm not at the gym to chat or to read the *New York Times*. I'm there to push myself and drip sweat.

Along similar lines . . . *How are you using your time during your job search?* Are you watching MTV while sending networking emails? Are you chatting through gmail while doing employer research? Are you taking a break every 10 minutes to check your Facebook page?

If you approach your job search with the same lack of focus and nonexistent intensity that most people bring to exercise, then be prepared for a long, painful job search. On the other hand, if you use your time wisely, you will get your dream job much faster.

The majority of time during your job search should be spent networking (i.e., communicating and meeting with people who could hire you or refer you). You'll learn what networking is (and what it is not) in greater detail later in this chapter. Don't be like most job-seekers and spend most of your time updating your résumé or applying for advertised jobs. There are much more valuable things on which to spend your time.

> LEIBMAN LIFE LESSON:
> *Do not assume time spent toward your goal equals progress made toward your goal.*

The #1 objective of this chapter is to help you be strategic with all your job search efforts, so that you can get hired as quickly as possible. In addition to sharing more job search time-management secrets and schooling you on what networking is (and what it is not), this chapter will teach you the following:

► How to identify the abundance of resources you already have on your side

► How to identify the best (and worst) networking events to attend

► How to create a strategy for using LinkedIn and other websites to get hired faster

## WHAT IS NETWORKING?

I keep saying that networking is the #1 way to get hired, but you may be thinking, "I still don't really know what networking is!" It's certainly a term that used to confuse me.

When I was a student, there is no way I would have thought I'd be writing a book less than 10 years later as an advocate for networking. During my teenage years, I was painfully shy, and I assumed networking was all about being fake and able to schmooze with rich, successful people you didn't know. I thought networking was a practice used only by the elite and powerful—a group I was not part of.

I grew up in one of the wealthiest counties in the United States in an extremely affluent suburb in Long Island, New York, called Garden City. However, the truth is that my family lived on the first block of town, as opposed to the mansions on the other side of town that looked like houses from *MTV Cribs*, and my parents were educators. We certainly didn't have problems paying bills, but I also didn't get a BMW or Hummer for my 16th birthday, as many kids in town did.

I resented the idea of networking initially because I thought it was a process I was not allowed to tap into. What I learned was the opposite. Networking is nothing more than a *lifelong process of building friendships*. (In contrast, what I call Job Search Networking is the process of generating job leads, referrals, and information from other people.)

Networking is for anyone and everyone. If you are generous, reliable, and willing to put in the effort needed to build relationships, you can be great at networking. This is true no matter where you are from and no matter what your personality is. Like anything, networking also gets much easier with practice. Let me clear up a few more misconceptions I had about networking, since you might have them as well.

► *Networking is NOT "a sign of weakness."* There is no such thing as a self-made man or woman. Life is a team sport. Kobe Bryant has teammates and coaches, and Tom Brady has teammates and coaches. In other words, even the world's greatest athletes got to where they are with help from other people. It is not a sign of weakness to rely on networking, especially at the start of your career. Networking is a sign of strength. It's an admission and acceptance of the fact that you don't have all the answers. It's delusional to think you can get where you want to be on your own, especially when you are young and when you aim high.

► *Networking is NOT "collecting business cards."* Another mistake inexperienced networkers make is to think networking is about just collecting business cards. Several years ago, I attended a networking event with a colleague. Before the event, he challenged me to a contest to see who could collect more business cards that evening. I declined. There's nothing wrong with trying to meet a lot of people, but never pursue quantity over quality. One meaningful, strategic interaction with the right person will provide much more value than 10 superficial conversations with people who lack hiring authority or who will never remember you.

► *Networking is NOT "annoying to other people."* How would you feel if someone sent you an email, told you she admired you, and asked for some of your advice on how she could be like you in the future? Would you get angry? Would you be annoyed? Of course not. Here's the truth: When done correctly and genuinely, networking is flattering to other people. This does not mean that everyone will welcome your requests for advice, but I have found that most people (especially really successful people) love to share their success secrets and tell their stories.

► *Networking is NOT "cheating."* When I interviewed with the Washington Wizards as a student in college, the people there didn't say, "You know one of our former senior executives, huh? Well, in that case, there is no need to interview you. You're hired!" Instead, their thought process was: "You know one of our former senior executives, huh? In that case, we'll take a look at your résumé and give you a chance to come in for an interview to prove why we should hire you." Networking is not nepotism. Do people get hired sometimes just because of whom they are related to or whom they know personally? Of course. However, that's not what I'm trying to teach you here. Networking is just how you get a chance to sell yourself. There is nothing unethical about this strategy. It's usually the only way you will get a chance to prove why you deserve your dream job.

► *Networking is NOT "something you do only when you need a job or favor."* If you try to connect with people only when you need something, you might get away with it initially, but it will catch up with you quickly. Networking is something you must do throughout your career. Again, networking is a *lifelong* process of building friendships.

► *Networking is NOT "all about whom you know."* Most people think networking is all about the people you know. They are wrong. Some people think networking is all about who knows you. They are also wrong.

Here's the truth: Networking is all about *who likes you and who respects you.* Before referring you to someone else, a successful

> **LEIBMAN LIFE LESSON:**
> *Networking is not about whom you know or who knows you. Networking is all about who likes you and who respects you.*

person is consciously or subconsciously asking herself, "Do I like and respect this person enough to put my reputation on the line by introducing her to someone I trust?" If the answer is "no," networking will get you nowhere. However, if the answer is "yes," a young job-seeker can usually get almost anyone to open his Rolodex.

The good news is that it does not take years of rapport-building to get someone to like you and respect you, and it is incredibly easy to stand out in a good way. You just need to make someone confident that you will represent him well if he puts his reputation on the line by introducing you to his contacts. For example, one of the executives influential in helping me get my dream job in the NBA was someone I spoke to for less than three minutes in person. I simply introduced myself to him the right way at a networking event. The result? He connected me with five of his best contacts after we spoke briefly on the phone the next week. I'd be willing to bet he had some family members (i.e., people he "knew" very well) that he would not have been willing to do that for.

## HOW TO GET ANYONE TO LIKE YOU AND RESPECT YOU RIGHT AWAY

If you want people to like you, you have to *like them first*. Take a second right now and write down the names of five of your favorite people. Look at that list one by one, and ask yourself if those people like you. I bet they do. We like people who genuinely like us.

If you want people to like you, you also have to get them to realize *you are like them*. Look at that list of people again. Are those people like you in some way? They probably have similar values, have similar passions, come from similar backgrounds, etc. We like people who are like us. Any time you reach out to someone new, try to establish some sort of genuine commonality immediately. One of the best ways to build real rapport is through a shared connection (you have a common friend) or through a shared affiliation (e.g., you both went to the same college, are from the same town, are part of the same church).

As I just wrote, networking is not about whom you know or who knows you. Unfortunately, there are people I "know" whom I would never refer to my top contacts because either (a) I don't like them or (b) I don't completely respect them. This might sound harsh, but I guard my reputation very carefully (you should also), and other referral sources will have a similar mindset. To be liked and respected, you must be:

► *Real.* Is this clear yet? Be comfortable with yourself and be genuine. Networking is not about being phony, slick, or fake. Insincere flattery will get you nowhere. Do you like it when people are artificial with you? Of course not. Just treat people with respect and be yourself. I wasn't smooth when I went to networking events in college, but I was authentic.

► *Enthusiastic.* Enthusiasm is contagious. Remember *The Lemonade Stand Principle* (from Chapter 2). People will be motivated to help you if you have a great attitude.

► *Curious.* Do you want to know the #1 way to impress people and build rapport quickly? Ask great questions. When you show interest in another person's opinion, you immediately become more likable. When you ask thought-provoking questions, you appear to be more intelligent. Networking is not about having a slick elevator pitch (another example of common career advice that is wrong) or telling other people about all of your achievements. It's also not about asking people for a job within two minutes of meeting them. Build rapport first by being curious and interested. Job leads and referrals will only come *after* you pass the likability/respect "test."

► *Appreciative.* Do you want to know the fastest way to be an annoying networker? Take people for granted. You always want to try to give first or to return a favor somehow, but the greatest gift you can give someone is your genuine appreciation.

► *Professional.* If you look like a slob or if your Facebook page would make Snooki blush, you will not be referred to other people, no matter how talented or likable you may be. You also have to be reliable. If you schedule a time to get career advice from someone on the phone and you miss the call, you may be able to reschedule a call. However, you will have blown any chance of getting a referral.

> **LEIBMAN LIFE LESSON:**
> *You are a representation of the people in your network, so represent them well. If networking is not working for you, it might be because of how you are presenting yourself to other people.*

# LEIBMAN'S LEXICON FOR JOB SEARCH NETWORKING

Now that we have discussed what networking is and what networking is not, let's discuss the different types of Job Search Networking and some other key terms you need to understand. (Appendix A in the back of this book also provides a glossary with all the career success terms I define throughout the book.)

► *Affiliations* are organizations you are a member of through your personal life, your academic life, or your professional life. This includes any religious groups, athletic leagues, social clubs, volunteer groups, academic institutions, honor societies, Greek organizations, professional associations, etc.

► *Level 1 Contacts* are people you already know, such as your friends, family, or professional contacts.

► *Level 2 Contacts* are people you do not know (yet), but who have something in common with you. You could both know the same person, or you could both be part of a specific group. Level 2 Contacts are "hidden" contacts, and most people never take the time to find them.

► *Level 3 Contacts* are people you do not know (yet) who do not share any common connections or affiliations with you.

► *Game-Changers* are successful senior executives in your ideal industry with the power to hire you or the ability to influence other people with the power to hire you. Game-Changers can be Level 1 Contacts, Level 2 Contacts, or Level 3 Contacts.

► *Warm Networking* is the process of connecting with your Level 1 Contacts (people you already know), while also using your Level 1 Contacts and your Affiliations to connect with your Level 2 Contacts (people you have something in common with). This is called Warm Networking because you are likely to get a warm, positive response from people you know and people you have something in common with.

▶ *Cool Networking* is the process of *introducing yourself in person* to Level 3 Contacts who are Game-Changers. This is called Cool Networking because you are less likely to get a positive response than with Warm Networking. Having said that, I got my dream job in the NBA through Cool Networking, so it can still be very effective, when done correctly. (Cool Networking is what most people think of when they hear the word "networking.")

▶ *Cold Networking* is the process of *introducing yourself via phone or the Internet* to Level 3 Contacts who are Game-Changers. This is called Cold Networking because you are least likely to get a positive response from this form of networking.

▶ *Advice Appointments* are 15- to 30-minute appointments (in person or on the phone) when you get to interview Game-Changers for advice on breaking into a certain field. Advice Appointments are not "Informational Interviews." (You may be more familiar with that term.) While Informational Interviews are used to determine *if* you want to pursue a certain field, Advice Appointments are used to get advice after you have already decided what you want to do. (We'll discuss Advice Appointments in detail in Chapter 6.)

▶ *Insider Information* is information provided by a Game-Changer about best-practices for breaking into an industry. Insider Information also includes information about trends or best-practices for a certain field. You can also get Insider Information through a variety of online sources that will be covered later in this chapter. To be 100 percent clear, I'm not talking about anything illegal, like insider secrets on stocks. I'm just talking about insights that are generally not known by people outside an industry.

In order to get your dream job as quickly as possible, you should use Warm Networking, Cool Networking, and Cold Networking. The ultimate goal of any form of networking is to line up

Advice Appointments with Game-Changers. When you connect with enough Game-Changers in the right fashion, you will get Insider Information and learn about "hidden" job opportunities.

Last point on networking for now: Do whatever you can to meet people *in person*, regardless of what type of contact they are or how you get connected. This is extremely important! Something magical happens when you meet someone face-to-face.

## ARE YOU TAKING YOUR EXISTING NETWORK FOR GRANTED?

When I was a student in college, I didn't think I knew anyone who could help me, so I looked for a job by myself. Even so, I eventually got a job with an NBA team because I networked successfully with people I did not know. However, I probably could have ended up in the same place (and saved myself a lot of time and energy) if I had done more to utilize the network I had as a college student.

Let me give you the specifics on my situation as proof of why you need to start with the people around you. One of my college roommates had a family friend who was a senior executive for the Verizon Center, the arena where the Washington Wizards played. He was an alumnus of my college, Johns Hopkins University (JHU), and he got us free tickets to a few Wizards games when we were seniors in college. I even met him at a game once, but I somehow never even thought to ask for his advice on my job search.

Another one of my best friends in college knew Wes Unseld Jr., the son of NBA Hall of Famer Wes Unseld Sr. Wes Sr. was GM for the Washington Wizards during my senior year in college, and Wes Jr. worked in the basketball operations office. Wes Jr. also graduated from JHU, but I failed to leverage that contact as well.

Before you spend any time looking for jobs or trying to get connected to new people, make a list of your current resources. You will probably be surprised to learn whom you already have on your side, and this personal network list will make your job search 10 times easier than trying to do it on your own like I did.

In general, your current network is composed of three groups.

(There will be some overlap between the groups.) Even a young job-seeker should be able to generate a list of at least 100 people and a number of organizations that she is affiliated with by accessing the three networking groups.

## Networking Group 1: Personal Contacts (and Personal Affiliations)

Your family and friends will be your biggest advocates, and they probably know a lot of people who could help you. This group includes:

- ► Parents, siblings, and other family members

- ► Friends of family members

- ► Friends from your school, hometown, church, or other religious organization, sports teams/leagues, recreational activities, social clubs, volunteer activities, etc.

- ► Acquaintances and friends of friends

- ► Personal contacts through social media platforms (people you have "met" only through Facebook or other personal websites)

- ► Personal affiliations (organizations you participate in during your free time, such as a church or other religious group)

## Networking Group 2: Academic Contacts (and Academic Affiliations)

Even if you have already graduated from college, you still have hundreds of people (maybe even thousands of people) in your network because of your academic background. This group includes:

- ► Former/current classmates

- ► Career center at your college

- ► Former/current professors (and other professors on campus)

- ► Other campus staff

- ► Alumni of your school(s)

- ► Schools you have attended

- ► Honor societies you have been inducted into

- ► Fraternities and sororities you have been inducted into

- ► Other student groups/activities you are/were involved in

## Networking Group 3: Professional Contacts (and Professional Affiliations)

These can be contacts from part-time positions, internships, or full-time jobs. This group includes:

- ► Former bosses, colleagues, customers, vendors, and partners

- ► Current colleagues, customers, vendors, and partners (if you are currently employed, you need to be careful here. Your current employer will probably not be pleased if it learns you are looking for a new job.)

- ► Professional contacts through social media platforms (people you have "met" only through LinkedIn or other professional websites)

- ► Professional associations you are involved in

To maximize your contacts and affiliations, take the following three steps:

1. *Create a Current Contact List.* Make a list of all of the personal contacts, academic contacts, and professional contacts in your current network.

2. *Connect online.* Once you have identified all the people you already know, connect on Facebook with everyone. Then, sign in to your LinkedIn account (you created a LinkedIn profile after reading Chapter 4, right?) and send personalized invitations to connect there as well. (I'll show you why it is important to connect with everyone through Facebook and LinkedIn in Chapter 6. To be brief, those sites make it easier than ever before to connect with Game-Changers for career advice.)

3. *Make a list of your affiliations and any relevant resources/ events.* Go to the website for each of your personal, academic, and professional affiliations, and see if there is a "Careers" page. Make note of any relevant events worth attending, such as career workshops, career fairs, or alumni networking events. For example, nearly every college has a website for its career center, and most career centers offer a variety of professional development programs and events. These programs are usually free. Many colleges also have on-campus recruiting programs for students where top employers come to campus to conduct interviews for job openings. Ideally, you should look for events where you can meet people in person.

> LEIBMAN LIFE LESSON:
> *Do not take your existing network for granted! You probably have access to people right now who can help you get your dream job.*

## ALL NETWORKING EVENTS ARE *NOT* CREATED EQUAL

As defined earlier in the chapter, Cool Networking is the process of connecting *in person* with Level 3 Contacts who are Game-Changers. I am probably not the first person who has told you the importance of going to networking events. But most people have probably told you that you should be out there going to as many networking events as possible. That is another piece of career advice that is wrong!

Just like quantity of contacts is not as important as *quality* of contacts, the quantity of networking events is not as important as the *quality* of events. In other words, going to one highly targeted networking event makes a lot more sense than going to 10 generic networking events. There is always value in meeting new people, but most networking events are actually a waste of time.

Going to generic networking events to get your dream job is like going to bars to meet your ideal type of guy or girl. It's not very strategic. For example, if a guy wants to date girls who are devout Catholics, he is much better off getting involved in events at his church than going to bars (where he will have no idea which girls carry Bibles in their purses). Similarly, if a girl wants to date guys who love animals, she is much better off going to dog parks or animal rescue shelters than going to bars (where she will have no idea which guys like to play with puppies).

OK, back to networking. . . . The best networking events are usually not called "networking events." "Networking events" are usually just full of salespeople and people looking for jobs. Instead, the best "networking events" are industry conferences or other events that Game-Changers from your ideal industry will be attending for their own benefit. As a job-seeker, you need to go to these places, too.

You also need to look for other ways where you can "join" your industry and connect with Game-Changers. By "joining" an industry, you will also learn Insider Information, making yourself a very confident, competent networker and interviewer. In order to determine how you can join the industry you want to break into, you need to ask yourself the following questions:

► Where can I go in person to connect with Game-Changers?

► Where can I go online to connect with Game-Changers?

► What associations, conferences, or events will Game-Changers be attending?

▶ What information sources (e.g., newspapers, e-newsletters, online discussion groups, blogs, magazines, trade journals) will Game-Changers be following?

The first step for joining your industry is to identify the associations most relevant to your career. Every industry (or job function) has at least one major association. Associations can operate on an international, national, regional, state, and/or city/county level; international and national organizations usually have regional or state chapters as well. Most associations are open for anyone to join, and students and young professionals usually receive special membership discounts (sometimes as low as $25 to $50 for the year).

Consider joining a professional association if it is highly targeted to your career aspirations because it will be worth the small investment. You should also try to volunteer or take on a leadership role so that you can give first to the organization. Associations are always desperate for support. Here's proof. A year before publishing this book, I was asked if I would like to be *president* of a state association after attending *one* event as a nonmember!

By joining an association, you will instantly convert all of the organization's members into Level 2 Contacts because of your shared affiliation. In addition, you can often get access to the entire membership directory, which will be a terrific source of leads for Game-Changers.

You can visit your local library to get a copy of *The Encyclopedia of Trade Associations*, or you can identify relevant associations through www.google.com. Just search by relevant keywords for your ideal industry and/or job function and for conferences and events related to your ideal career.

You can also tighten your searches by a geographic location, or you can broaden your searches for just your industry or just your job function. The American Marketing Association was the organization hosting the networking event where I met a Game-Changer during my quest for my dream job in pro sports. This shows that there can still be a lot of value in attending events based on a job function, even if the association is not industry-specific. In fact, the benefit of participating in broader organizations is that you will meet people across a variety of industries, and there will be fewer people who want the same job you do. Just make sure not to go too broad, as most people do by attending standard "networking events."

Most associations have an annual conference or regular events where current/potential members can get together in person to exchange best-practices and build relationships. There are also conferences and events not affiliated with a specific association. For example, there are two annual conferences in March in Washington, D.C., for the sports industry, the Sports Events Marketing Experience (SEME) and the Sports Industry Networking and Career (SINC) conference. Most industry networking events, including these two, are open to anyone. (Again, there are conferences and associations for *every* industry and job function, so don't ignore this strategy if you want a career outside sports or marketing.)

> **LEIBMAN LIFE LESSON:**
> *If you want to break into an industry, you should "join" the industry first.*

## CRASH THE PARTY THROUGH LINKEDIN

As discussed earlier in this chapter, Cold Networking is the process of *introducing yourself (via phone or the Internet)* to Level 3 Contacts who are Game-Changers. This is where LinkedIn can really come in handy.

Google searches generally do not show you what is going on inside LinkedIn, although LinkedIn recently added a feature called "Open Groups," where some groups are now searchable on the web. (I anticipate that most groups will be "Open Groups" in the future.) With more than 100 million business professionals (and growing) on the site worldwide, LinkedIn is an essential tool for your job search and career. Many of the associations you identify will also have a LinkedIn group. While some LinkedIn groups are private, most LinkedIn groups are open to anyone. LinkedIn groups are fantastic sources of material on Game-Changers and Insider Information.

LinkedIn also has a lot of groups that have simply been started by people working in an industry or passionate about an industry. To join a group on LinkedIn, just click on the "Groups" tab at the top of your profile page and search for relevant groups. When you join a group, you will be brought to a page where you can determine your settings, so you can even have group updates emailed to you daily or weekly. You can also search for other types of groups through LinkedIn, such as:

- Groups for your college/alumni

- Groups for your desired job function

- Groups that are geographically relevant (i.e., your selected metro area)

- Groups for the associations you identified through your Google searches

- Groups for your ideal employers (many employers have their own LinkedIn groups)

*Bonus secret:* Look at LinkedIn profiles for Game-Changers in your ideal industry, and join groups they have already joined on LinkedIn. (Their groups are usually visible on their LinkedIn profiles.) Very few people know you can do this or think to do this.

While you can join up to 50 different groups on LinkedIn (the maximum LinkedIn allows per account), it is definitely not necessary to join that many. Just join those that are most relevant. Join some groups that are very large and join some groups that are highly targeted (i.e., a group limited by industry, job function, and geography).

# GET INSIDER INFORMATION ON YOUR OWN

Insider Information is immensely valuable for cracking the "hidden job market" and being a savvy interviewer. Insider Information can also help you advance your career after you get hired. In addition to talking to Game-Changers, here are five ways to use the latest online tools to become an industry insider on your own *before you actually work in an industry*. This is another reason why now is the best time ever to get your dream job. Insider Information is now more accessible to the general public than ever before.

1. *"Like" relevant Facebook fan pages.* Use Facebook to become a fan for your target market of employers and for relevant associations/groups/events. Most organizations have a Facebook button on their home pages. If not, you can just sign in to Facebook and enter the name of the organization you want to follow. By doing so, you will receive its status updates in your Facebook news feed (and you can view the pages on your own time as well).

2. *Follow relevant Twitter accounts.* Set up a free account at www.Twitter.com to follow your top employers, relevant associations, Game-Changers, and so on. If you are currently employed and looking to change jobs, you can also set up a Twitter account anonymously (don't use your real name or picture).

3. *Subscribe to relevant information sources.* Most organizations (employers or associations) have some sort of daily, weekly, or monthly newsletter (print or email) that updates customers, members, and fans on relevant news. Subscribe to the newsletter for each of your ideal employers and for any associations you identified above. Most newsletters are free and available for anyone. You should also do some additional Google searches for relevant publications or blogs. You don't need to sign up for every single publication for your ideal industry (there could be hundreds or thousands that are rele-

vant), so use your judgment on those that appear to be most comprehensive and popular among Game-Changers.

4. *Subscribe to relevant Google alerts.* Just like you did when you set up a "Google alert" for your name in Chapter 4, you can also set up Google alerts (at www.google.com/alerts) for each of your top employers and for any relevant associations, Game-Changers, or keywords you want to follow.

5. *Check out corporate "careers" pages.* Most employers have a "careers" page with details on available jobs and what the organization looks for in employees. While I do not encourage you to submit a résumé blindly through these pages (if you do that, your résumé will likely just end up in a black hole), these pages provide great information on what the company looks for, and they often show if the company is actively hiring for any relevant positions. Remember that employers are still passively hiring even if they are not actively hiring.

## IF YOU INSIST ON USING JOB BOARDS

With less than 10 percent of all jobs being filled through online job boards, spend little or no time on them (i.e., 15 minutes per day or one hour per week at the maximum). Ultimately, the only way job boards have any value is if you use them to identify opportunities and then you Apply Aggressively, as we'll discuss in Chapter 6.

If you insist on using job boards, do a few Google searches to find niche job boards relevant to your ideal career. There are niche job boards for all job functions and for all industries. You can also check out www.simplyhired.com, a free website that pulls listings from thousands of websites, including job boards, employer career pages, and more. Most job boards allow you to set up highly targeted email alerts so that you can be notified of relevant job opportunities as soon as they are posted online.

# JOB SEARCH Q&A WITH THE AUTHOR

Here are answers to some common questions from job-seekers about how to manage your time during a job search.

**Q:** I feel like I'm all over the place with my job search. Any tips on how I can be more organized in keeping track of everything?

**A:** Here are four secrets for staying organized as a job-seeker.

➤ *Set up a job search "office."* Find a location outside your home with Internet access (e.g., a local Starbucks or library) where you can conduct most of your job search activities. Trying to run a job search out of a dorm room, bedroom, or extra room in your home will not be fun for you or the people you live with. Also, go to an office supply store and buy some high-quality résumé paper, folders, a notebook, index cards, thank-you notes, envelopes, stamps, and a portfolio pad or briefcase. Having these items handy will make you much more efficient. Keep all your job search materials organized in one place. Then, when it's time to "visit the office," you have everything ready to go.

➤ *Do a weekly review and planning session.* At the end of each week (either on Friday afternoon or over the weekend), spend one to two hours reviewing the progress you made over the last week, and plan what you will do for your job search the following week. In particular, set three to five main goals for the next week and schedule appointments with yourself for when you will conduct your job search during the week. If you are fully employed right now, you may be able to devote only several hours during the upcoming week. However, by looking at the week in advance, you are much more likely to schedule and keep appointments with yourself. If you are out of work, treat your job search like a full-time job by spending 30 to 40 hours per week on getting a new job. What else do you have to do?! Remember: For each week you are unemployed, you could be losing $1,000 to $2,000 or more, depending on what your salary level is.

▶ *Develop a system for keeping track of your referral sources, contacts, and target employers.* When I serviced hundreds of accounts as a salesperson for the Washington Wizards, I used the "old-school" method of keeping track of my prospects and clients with index cards. Each person had her own index card, which featured notes from prior communications along with the dates for follow-ups. The index cards made it easy for me to skim through all my prospects during my weekly review session, when I would pluck out the people to follow up with the following week. For any follow-ups at specific times (i.e., scheduled calls or in-person meetings), use an online planner like Microsoft Outlook or a daily physical planner. This system worked very well for me, although you can certainly use a more sophisticated, 100 percent online method if you prefer (such as www.JibberJobber.com). You get only one chance to impress a referral source or potential employer, so you cannot afford to miss a call or forget to follow up when you said you would.

▶ *Save templates and documents.* Every communication you have with potential referral sources and employers *must* be customized during your job search. However, it can be very time-consuming to start from scratch every time you send a follow-up note or write a cover letter or email a new networking contact. So, if you are going to send an email or document more than one time, save a template somewhere on your computer. Then, you just have to personalize the message each time.

Q: I find myself getting distracted very easily. How can I stay focused during my job search?

**A:** Here are three secrets to staying focused as a job-seeker.

▶ *Track how you spend all your job search time.* I came up with this idea after reading a personal development treasure chest, *The Compound Effect* by Darren Hardy, publisher of *Success* magazine. In his book, Hardy talks about the value of tracking your behaviors. Tracking your time may sound like a lot of work, but it's not. Just keep a small notepad handy, and write down the categories and times for your activities (e.g., 10:00–11:30 a.m.: sent networking emails, 12:00–2:00 p.m.: lunch appointment with Jen Smith of ABC Company). Then, at the end of each day (and at the end of the week), you can review how you spent your time. This practice will be eye-opening.

▶ *Ask the "a.m./p.m. question."* I got this concept from Mark LeBlanc, author of *Growing Your Business!* While Mark teaches the "a.m./p.m. question" as a business development and time management strategy for entrepreneurs, here is how it works for job-seekers. Each morning, ask yourself the following question: *What am I going to do today to get my dream job?* (You should aim for three to five daily goals.) Then, each evening, ask yourself the following question: *What did I do today to get my dream job?* Daily accountability is very important for job-seekers. If you find through the p.m. question that you didn't do what you said you would do at the beginning of the day, don't beat yourself up over it. Just get back to work the following day.

▶ *Find a job search "teammate."* Every Monday at 10 a.m., I have a 30- to 60-minute progress report call with my entrepreneur "teammate." We each share wins and challenges from the last week, along with goals for the next week. You should do the same to keep yourself focused as a job-seeker. Either hire a professional career coach like me, or use a professor, friend, family member, or former boss or colleague. You could also just use another job-seeker. (If you do, buy him a copy of this book so you can go through it together.) Whomever you select, make sure the person has your best interests at heart, and make sure he has a winning mindset. Then, set a time to speak each week for anywhere from 30 to 60 minutes.

## Jennifer Davis* Got Her Dream Job with the U.S. State Department

Since I was young, I had a fascination with other countries and cultures. Going into college, I realized that I also had an acute interest in government policy and international relations. Thus, working at the State Department seemed like a natural fit. However, I quickly became disheartened. As an undergrad, I was rejected multiple times by the State Department internship program, which I had hoped to use as a springboard for employment. Undaunted, I realized I needed a new strategy.

During my last year of college, I started thinking about how the next few years of my professional life might play out. I talked to friends, professors, and young professionals and realized that most people in international relations held graduate degrees. Knowing my eventual goal, I took matters one step at a time: I decided to get some research experience working at a local financial services firm so that I could pad my grad school application. I also offered my services to a former professor who was working on a book and ended up getting credit as a contributing author.

I realized that I really needed to specialize in a given area, and I decided on the Middle East, both because of personal interest and its emerging status as a region of preeminent import. Thus, I began taking some preliminary Arabic lessons and reading up on regional politics. I also researched average GRE scores for the schools I was interested in and set personal targets for myself.

During graduate school, I realized that all the prep work I had done helped me both during grad school as well as with the post–grad

---

*Given the nature of her work, a pseudonym has been used.

school job search. I was able to leverage my experience to land various internships, and during my second semester, I finally became an intern in the State Department's Bureau of Near Eastern Affairs. Throughout graduate school, I met with my school's career services office, and I spent a summer in the Middle East doing research and Arabic language study. I was accepted into the Presidential Management Fellowship (PMF) program, which—along with the Foreign Service—is the State Department's primary recruiting tool, and I ended up getting a job through contacts that my school's career services office set up for me.

I would strongly encourage you to have a plan. I didn't have every single aspect worked out, but I knew where I wanted to be. I laid out my various goals and what I would need to do to achieve those goals. Also, I would highly encourage you to work with your school's career services office. The alumni contacts and guidance that it can provide you are invaluable, so get connected with this office early.

I got my dream job and so can you!

—JENNIFER DAVIS

# CHAPTER 6

# LOOK

## (STEP # 5)

> "Things do not happen. Things are made to happen."
>
> —JOHN F. KENNEDY, 35TH PRESIDENT OF THE UNITED STATES

**April 12, 2003: at Johns Hopkins University (in my dorm room)**

I got up early, showered, and put on my finest (i.e., only) business suit. Then, I woke up one of my roommates. Since I was unable to knot my own tie at that point of my life, I needed my friend to do it for me. It was 8 a.m. on a Saturday, so he was not pleased.

The Baltimore chapter of the American Marketing Association was hosting a career workshop for local students that morning, and one of the featured speakers was a senior executive from Fila named Howe Burch. My only goal in attending the event was to introduce myself to Mr. Burch and ask for his advice on how I could break into the sports marketing industry. The thought of doing this would never have crossed my mind several months earlier, but my growing desperation had made me more resourceful and proactive.

As I drove to the event, I rehearsed the conversation out loud that I hoped we would have. Networking was not something that came naturally to me, and I could not afford to botch this encounter.

I was nervous, but I was optimistic. As I approached the event location, I thought to myself: *"Maybe this will be the break I need."*

Midway through the event, I found Mr. Burch, stuck out my hand, looked him right in the eye, and said, "Mr. Burch, you are the reason I came here today." It was the truth, and I could tell that he knew I was genuine based on how he looked back at me. "My dream is to work in sports marketing after college," I continued. "Would it be possible for me to ask you a few questions?"

While he was friendly, we spoke for less than two minutes since it was during a break. Then he gave me his business card and told me to email him so that we could chat another time.

I did what he told me to do.

Immediately after the event ended, I drove back to my house, grabbed my job search materials, and went straight to the library. There were many other students who had approached Mr. Burch that day, so my goal was to be the first one to follow up with him.

We spoke on the phone the next week. At the end of our 15-minute conversation, he said, "Pete, I'll check with some of my contacts and let you know if I hear of any openings."

Again, being driven by desperation, I got a little bolder than I would have been several months earlier: "Mr. Burch, would it be easier for you if I reached out to some of your contacts on your behalf instead?"

"I like that idea, Pete," he replied. "Write down these five names, phone numbers, and email addresses, and tell them I sent you."

I did what he told me to do.

The following week, I spoke on the phone with one of those referrals, a man named David Cope. Mr. Cope had a sports consulting business and he had worked for nearly every pro sports team in Washington, D.C., and Baltimore. At the end of that call, he said, "Pete, I know the director of sales for the Washington Wizards. Send him an email and tell him I sent you. I'd be willing to bet they'd bring you in for an interview. Then, it's up to you to sell yourself."

> **LEIBMAN LIFE LESSON:**
> *No one is going to deliver your dream job to your dorm room. You have to go out and get it.*

I did what he told me to do.

Four weeks later, I started my dream job.

The #1 objective of this chapter is to share the do's, don'ts, and secrets for success for the four best job search strategies (Warm Networking, Cool Networking, Cold Networking, and Applying Aggressively for advertised jobs). This is the longest, richest chapter in this book, so go through it carefully.

## A SALESPERSON: TO BE OR NOT TO BE?

What image pops into your head when you hear the word "salesperson"? If you are like most people, you probably think back to some time you dealt with a sloppy guy with a thick moustache who tried to jam a product or service down your throat. Given the behavior and demeanor of the typical salesperson, most people have a negative perception of sales. I certainly did when I was in college.

However, after becoming the #1 salesperson for an NBA franchise, I realized that the best salespeople are not pushy or slimy. The best salespeople have integrity and are very adept at building relationships and friendships.

Here are seven of the greatest lessons I have learned about sales. Keep these in mind during your job search and as you apply/interview for jobs.

1. *Your batting average does not matter, so swing often and swing for the fences.* In my last three years working for the Washington Wizards, I had more prospects ignore my emails/calls or tell me "no" (or something worse) than anyone else in the company. I also sold five to 10 times as much as most of my colleagues. As a job-seeker, you need to approach your search the same way. Do not take rejection personally. Just keep swinging. Assume that each "no" gets you closer to a "yes," and assume that each "no" is independent. In other words, just because one person says "no" does not mean the next person can't say "yes." Keep your pipeline of leads full

so that you are not overly dependent on any one networking contact or job lead. The more options you have, the better. You still want to treat each lead with care, but having lots of options takes the pressure off you in each interaction. This will make you more relaxed and more confident. You'll also appear less desperate.

2. *Conviction is convincing.* You should know more about your product than anyone else. If you don't believe in the value of what you are selling (in this case, that's you), why should other people? The goal is to be confident (not cocky) and enthusiastic (not desperate). You also want employers to think that you have other options. I'm not telling you to lie or to be a blatant name-dropper. Instead, find subtle ways to drop hints that other organizations are considering you as well. Employers want to hire people who are in high demand, and they will often pay more for job-seekers who appear to have plenty of employment options.

3. *Don't focus on the sale; just focus on the next step.* Getting hired, like making any sale, is a process. As a job-seeker, you always need to be thinking to yourself, *"What is my goal for this action?"* and *"What is the next step in this process?"* You always have to take the lead and stay one step ahead, whether it's in a networking conversation, an Advice Appointment, or a job interview. Never leave follow-up to chance or to some-one else. If you consistently try to move to the next step in the process of getting your dream job, you will eventually get where you want to be.

4. *A soft sell is much more effective than a hard sell.* The trade-mark and mantra of America's #1 sales authority, Jeffrey Gitomer, is "People don't like to be sold, but they love to buy!" Remember this throughout your job search. Unless an employer is publicly advertising a job opening (we'll cover that later in the chapter), be subtle in your approach. Starting a conversation by asking someone you don't know if his orga-nization is hiring is like walking up to a stranger on the street

and asking if she is looking for a new mate! There are much better ways to break the ice.

5. *Don't ask for jobs; ask for* advice. There are a variety of reasons why this is really important. First, if you ask someone for a job before demonstrating your worth, you will usually be met with a stall tactic (e.g., "Send your résumé to HR") or a flat-out rejection (e.g., "We are not hiring now"). The stall tactic sends you to the black hole with every schmo trying to get a job. The rejection leaves you no next step, other than a lame response like, "Well, can I follow up with you in the future?"

   Another reason why it's foolish to ask if an organization is hiring is because every great employer is *always* hiring when the right person comes along! As I mentioned in Chapter 1, if someone tells you her organization is not hiring, she either does not want to hire *you*, or she is not the final decision-maker.

   When you ask for *advice*, you invite someone into a low-pressure conversation, and you can still find out how hiring works for an organization/industry. A subtle approach also makes it easier to earn referrals to other people who can help you get where you want to be.

6. *Mass communication efforts are worthless when you are selling a premium product.* Mass emails and other forms of non-personalized communication (i.e., sending letters "to whom it may concern") provide no value when selling any high-end product (in this case, that's you). Do not send mass emails asking your network for any form of help. *Every* communication during your job search needs to be one-to-one and personalized, even when communicating with people you know. If you send an email blast saying something like, "Hey everyone, let me know if you hear of any job openings," very few people (even friends and family) will take the initiative to email you back and see how they can help. Instead, most people will assume someone else will respond. This is known as "diffusion of responsibility." On the other hand, it's hard

to ignore someone asking you for help individually.

7. *It is not always wise to be different.* Standing in Times Square with a poster that says "Hire me!" is being different *in a bad way.* You don't want to get someone's attention by looking desperate. Be different in a good way.

> **LEIBMAN LIFE LESSON:**
>
> *Approach your job search like a great salesperson, and you will get your dream job faster and with less effort.*

## DO YOU KNOW HOW TO ASK FOR DIRECTIONS?

Imagine that you are parked in your car at a red light at a busy intersection. I pull up in my car right next to you. I honk my horn, roll down the window, and look at you. You notice that I am trying to get your attention, so you roll your window down and look at me. Here is the conversation that follows:

**PETE:** Excuse me. I'm lost. Would you mind giving me some directions?

**YOU:** Sure. Where are you trying to go?

**PETE:** Well . . . I'm really flexible. It doesn't matter. I'll go anywhere. Where do you think I should go?

Sounds crazy, right? You would have no idea how to respond to such a ridiculous question because you could send me in a hundred different directions. No one would do this, right?

Well, unfortunately, this is how most people approach Job Search Networking! They go to their friends, family, and other contacts and say something like, "In this economy, I'll take any job I can get. It doesn't matter. I'm really flexible. Do you know of any job openings?"

I get emails like this all the time (note: Saying you want "any job in marketing" is not much better), and I have to admit that this is how I conducted my job search when I decided to leave the NBA in 2008. One senior executive politely told me that he could not help me until I told him where I wanted to go.

This is one reason why Chapter 3 is so important, so go back through that chapter again if you still are unsure what you want to do. People will not be inspired to help you (or hire you) if you have no purpose or focus for your job search. More important, they won't know *how* to help you.

All of the people featured as success stories in this book (myself included) got very clear on where they wanted to go *before* they looked for jobs. This is extremely important no matter what job search strategy you utilize.

> LEIBMAN LIFE LESSON:
>
> *Networking for your dream job is not complicated.*
> *Find people who have been where you want to be, ask them how they got there, and ask them how you can get there.*

When asking for directions, don't be a "hitchhiker," either. You should not be asking people to send your résumé out for you or to do any other part of your job search for you. Ask people how *you* can take yourself where you want to be. The more work you create for another person, the less likely he will be motivated to help you, even if he likes you and respects you.

## JOB SEARCH STRATEGY #1: WARM NETWORKING

When it comes to warm networking, there is good news and bad news. Let me explain . . .

### The Good News About Warm Networking

Almost all job-seekers ignore their Level 1 and Level 2 Contacts altogether. This is a *huge* mistake. Again, Level 1 Contacts are people you already know, and Level 2 Contacts are "hidden" contacts who share a common connection or affiliation with you.

Let's do some quick math to prove how important your Level 1 and Level 2 Contacts are to your job search. Let's say you have 100 Level 1 Contacts, and let's also say that each of those people knows 100 people whom you don't know. That means you are only an introduction away from 10,000 people! What if you know 200 people and each of those people knows 200 people you don't know? That means you are only an introduction away from 40,000 people! Get the point? Don't look *just* at the people you know. Understand that your contacts know lots of other people you don't know. Your network is so much bigger than you could possibly imagine. However, there is a catch. . . .

## The Bad News About Warm Networking

I invest more time and energy into networking than the large majority of my friends and contacts. I have a passion for people, I enjoy staying in touch, and I also understand the importance of networking as a *lifelong process*. However, I would be lying if I told you that I knew where more than 25 percent of my contacts work right now *and* where they have worked in the past. No one else knows this either. Let me explain.

Most of the people I know are people I met outside work (e.g., through college, church, sports leagues, and the gym). As a result, even though I know these people, I still have no idea where most of them actually work right now (very few people can clearly explain their jobs!) or what they have done for work in the past. As a result, if you were to come to me and say something like, "Hey Pete, do you know anyone who works for Google now or who used to work for Google?" my honest answer would be, "I don't know."

Can you have success if you go to your contacts and ask if they know anyone working in a certain industry or working for a certain employer? Sure, it's much better than having no direction at all, like most job-seekers. However, you are putting the pressure on your Level 1 Contacts to know where all of their contacts work, and that is a huge mistake. Luckily, there is now a better way to approach your Warm Networking.

## Using LinkedIn and Facebook in Warm Networking

Social media platforms like LinkedIn and Facebook operate as Rolodexes that get automatically updated for you. When people change jobs, they usually don't tell everyone they know, but they usually do update their social media profiles. As a result, by connecting with your contacts through LinkedIn and Facebook (you did that after reading Chapter 5, right?), you can research where your Level 1 and Level 2 Contacts work now *and* where they have worked in the past.

This is absolutely revolutionary!

Just five years ago, it was extremely cumbersome to learn and keep track of the backgrounds of your Level 1 and Level 2 Contacts. Now, you can view their *entire employment histories* online. This is another reason why now is the best time in history (seriously) to get your dream job. It's easier than ever before to tap into the "six degrees of separation" phenomenon.

The more well-connected you are through Facebook and LinkedIn, the easier it will be to get connected with people working for your ideal employers. As a result, when you "ask for directions," you can now say something like, "Hey Pete, I noticed you are connected on LinkedIn to a woman named Jackie Carroll who works for Google. How do you know her? Could you connect me with her so I could ask her for some career advice?" (For the record, this is a hypothetical example.)

Let's go over three little-known secrets on how to use LinkedIn and Facebook to make it even easier to get where you want to be.

### Using LinkedIn to Find Relevant Level 1 and Level 2 Contacts

You might not realize that you have a Level 1 Contact connected to one of your ideal employers. In addition, your Level 1 Contacts might not realize they can introduce you to someone relevant whom they know (your Level 2 Contacts). You can overcome this challenge by running an advanced search through your LinkedIn account for your ideal employers. Let's say that one of your ideal employers is Google. You could sign in to your LinkedIn account and enter "Google" in the search box for "Company," select "Current or past" to find current or past employees, and select "1st Connections" and "2nd Connections" for "Relationships." (LinkedIn refers to Level 1 Contacts and Level 2 Contacts as 1st Connections and 2nd Connections, respectively.)

This search will generate a list of all of your Level 1 and Level 2 Contacts on LinkedIn who work for Google now or have worked for Google in the past. In addition, for your Level 2 Contacts, this search will even show you whom you know in common with the Level 2 Contact (which LinkedIn refers to as "shared connections").

Last point on this: LinkedIn has recently been increasing its privacy features, so you might find that last names are not shown for certain people appearing in search results. If you run into that problem, you can then use www.Jigsaw.com to find someone's last name and complete contact information.

In addition to looking for Level 1 and Level 2 Contacts in your top employers, you can also look for other Level 2 Contacts working for relevant organizations (i.e., organizations in your ideal industry that are not on your target employer list). Here's how you do that. If you and I were connected on LinkedIn and you clicked on my profile, you would be brought to a summary of my profile. At the bottom left of the summary box for my profile, you will see the word "Connections." If you click that, you will be brought to another page that lists everyone I am connected to on LinkedIn, including the names, titles, and employers of each of my contacts. In other words, you can see my entire "Rolodex" on LinkedIn. It is possible to make your connections "private," but few people do.

Again, this is huge!

Then, you could scroll through all of my connections to see whom I know, and you could proactively ask me for an introduction to a specific person. It will probably not be efficient to do this for each of your contacts because of the time commitment involved, but it is worth it to scroll through the "LinkedIn Rolodexes" of your best advocates or most relevant connections.

### Using LinkedIn to Find Alumni Working for Your Ideal Employers

As we discussed, someone is a Level 2 Contact if he shares an affiliation with you, such as being an alumnus from your college. However, LinkedIn does not have the functionality to classify people this way. As a result, people who went to the same college as you can show up in LinkedIn as "3rd Connections" or "Out of your network," even though they meet my definition of a Level 2 Contact.

You also have thousands of Level 2 Contacts just from your affiliation with your college or university. You can use LinkedIn to find alumni from your college who currently or previously worked for your target employers. Just use the same search we used with our earlier example for Google, but include the name of your college in the "School" section and search for "All LinkedIn members" instead of "1st Connections" and "2nd Connections." As an example, I did a search for current or past employees of Google who also went to my alma mater, Johns Hopkins University. Through this search in 2011, I found 77 employees *currently* working for Google who attended JHU, and I also found 45 JHU alumni who used to work for Google!

### Using Facebook to Find Relevant Level 1 and Level 2 Contacts

Facebook can also help you identify people affiliated with your ideal employers. Just type in the name of an employer through Facebook's "People Search" feature. You can also refine your search by a city/region or by your alma mater. Since Facebook has five to six times as many users as LinkedIn, this is a great way to find additional Level 1 and Level 2 Contacts currently or previously employed by your top employers. (The reason to use LinkedIn as well is because LinkedIn's search features are much more user-friendly than the search features Facebook had at the time this book was published.)

These efforts might seem like a lot of work, but they will save you time in the end. The payoff will be much better than if you go to your contacts and ask if they "know anyone you can speak to." (If you don't identify any leads through these social media searches, then feel free to ask for introductions in the more traditional method.)

Regardless of whether you identify a contact through a social media website, you should reach out to people through email or by phone instead. Most people check their personal or work email addresses and phone numbers much more often than their social media accounts, and many people prefer not to be contacted through Facebook and LinkedIn by people they do not know.

## JOB SEARCH STRATEGY #2: COOL NETWORKING

Cool Networking is what most people think of when they hear the word *networking*. If networking with strangers intimidates you, take some solace in the fact that most people squirm at the thought of hanging out with people they don't know. Here are seven secrets for success with Cool Networking.

### Have a Strategy

As mentioned in Chapter 5, the average "networking event" is a poor use of time. Make sure you are going to the right events, and make sure you go to each event with a specific goal. Research anyone who might be in attendance (e.g., featured speakers or leadership from the organization hosting the event) and be prepared to ask a few intelligent, personalized questions about each person's work or her opinion on a topic related to her career. While small talk is inevitable at any networking event, the best conversations should go beyond the weather or the latest sporting event. Asking great questions (that you thought of in advance) is one of the best ways to stand out and make a great first impression.

## Show Up with the Right Mindset and Expectations

Most people put way too much pressure on themselves at networking events. No one is going to offer you a job on the spot anyway, so why go in with such an unrealistic expectation? Rather than going with the goal of getting a job, just look at a networking event as a way to meet new people, to learn, to exchange ideas, or to gain advice. Going to a networking event looking for a job is like going to a bar looking for a boyfriend or girlfriend! It puts unnecessary pressure on you, and this apprehension will have a negative impact on all of your interactions.

## Know What to Say

Other than asking your name, the first question you are asked at any event is what type of work you do. You do not want to improvise your answer. Make sure you prepare a concise, clear, and compelling way to introduce yourself. I call this an "elegant elevator pitch." You can reference some sort of academic, volunteer, or part-time project you are working on that is relevant. Your "pitch" at a networking event should be only five to 10 seconds long (maximum). Shorter is better. Despite what many people will tell you, an initial 30-second elevator pitch for yourself is completely unrealistic and will turn people off in a networking situation. (Save the longer pitch for a job interview.) Same goes for a summary of your achievements. The best way to impress people is not by bragging. It's by asking smart questions, by making a great first impression with your attitude, presentation, and body language, and by selling yourself subtly *when people ask you questions.*

Create a list of five to 10 questions you can use to break the ice at any event. Remember: The goal is to build rapport with the other person first. Here are some sample questions that you can personalize based on your career goals and the event you attend:

► How long have you been involved with _____, and how did you decide to get involved?

- How did you get your start in _____?

- How did you decide that you wanted to pursue your current career?

- What do you enjoy most about your work?

- What projects are you most excited about for the next year at your employer?

- How do you see _____ changing over the next few years?

- How do you think _____ has changed over the last few years?

- What advice would you have for someone looking to break into _____?

## Talk to Strangers

In general, you always want to attend a networking function with the goal of connecting with a specific person or people. However, these icebreakers can be valuable for connecting with other people at an event:

- *Break the ice at registration.* Introduce yourself to the person at the registration table and tell him that it is your first time attending the event. He will likely introduce you to several people. (You can also offer ahead of time to volunteer at the registration table.)

- *Break the ice through the host.* Introduce yourself to the person in charge of the organization hosting the event. This person probably knows most of the people in the room, and she is likely a very friendly person who would welcome the opportunity to introduce you to others.

- *Break the ice through food.* Look for an opportunity to break the ice with someone grabbing something to eat or drink.

▶ *Break the ice with someone else who looks lost.* Look for someone else who also seems to be alone, and walk over and introduce yourself.

▶ *Break the ice through a group.* Walk up to a group of three or more people and ask if you can join them. You have to use good judgment, however. If the people in the group are huddled very closely in a tight circle, take that as a sign that they are not receptive to including other people.

▶ *Break the ice before you arrive.* This is my favorite way to break the ice. You email key people before the event and say how excited you are to meet them at the event. No one ever does this, so it's a great way to stand out, especially if you want to connect with a speaker who will be swarmed with people trying to meet her at the event.

## Behave Professionally

Avoid alcohol altogether, or stick to one drink at most (assuming you are of legal drinking age). More than that will only increase your chances of doing something unprofessional. Unless you attend a breakfast, lunch, or dinner where it would be rude not to eat the meal being served, *never* eat anything at a networking event. There are too many things that could go wrong. For instance, you could spill Swedish meatball gravy on your shirt. Gross.

## Ask for the Next Step

As discussed earlier in the chapter, you always need to be thinking about getting to the next step in the process of getting your dream job. Upon meeting someone at a networking event, your goal should be to make enough of a connection to follow up for an Advice Appointment. At the end of a conversation (which could be after speaking for as little as one to two minutes or for more than 15 minutes), ask if you can follow up, if it makes sense. Just say something like, "I really enjoyed talking to you and would love to get some more of your advice if I could. Would it be possible for me to _____ (e.g., take you out for a cup of coffee, call you on the phone, send you an email), in order to ask you a few more questions?" Once you have already met in person, it's fine to shift the dialogue over to the phone.

## Follow Up Correctly

Many people go to networking events, participate in conversations with others, grab a few business cards, . . . and then they do absolutely nothing! This is among the biggest networking mistakes you could make. Make it your practice to follow up within one business day whenever you meet someone. Otherwise, it's easy to forget to follow up, and it's easy for people to forget you. At the minimum, send thank-you notes to anyone who gave you career advice, connect with your new contacts on LinkedIn, and add them to the contact management system you should have created after reading Chapter 5 (you read the Q&A section, right?). If a next step makes sense at this time, request it immediately.

> LEIBMAN LIFE LESSON:
>
> *Networking will not work*
> *without great*
> *follow-up.*

## JOB SEARCH STRATEGY #3: COLD NETWORKING

If you are going to contact people you don't know through the Internet or by phone, you must be very strategic. Here are some secrets for connecting with Game-Changers through Cold Networking.

## Don't Waste Your Time with HR

HR executives rarely have the final say in a hiring decision, and many have very little input at all. (I never even spoke to anyone in HR during the process of getting my dream job in the NBA or during my job search in 2008 when I landed multiple six-figure job offers.) Instead, HR departments usually serve as "bouncers" whose primary goal is to keep unwanted people "out of the club." This happens because the real hiring decision-makers (the people running departments and divisions in the organization) don't have time to weed through all the potential candidates. However, even if the HR executive does have a say in a hiring decision, the other reason it's not worth contacting him "cold" is because he is too obvious a target. If you are pursuing a popular organization or industry, there could be hundreds of other people harassing the HR department for jobs and career advice. Therefore, never go out of your way to connect with HR employees, unless you have a personal connection to them (or you want to work in the HR department).

## Don't Waste Your Time at the Bottom

If you know someone at the bottom of the organizational chart (i.e., an entry-level employee) at one of your target employers, feel free to contact her for advice during your job search. However, when it comes to Cold Networking, do not target young professionals. Young professionals can offer insights as to what entry-level jobs are like, but they won't have much pull in getting you hired or referred to the real decision-makers.

Again, you want to connect with Game-Changers. Successful senior executives generally have many more connections, much deeper industry knowledge, and a lot more influence in hiring decisions. They are also much more likely to want to help you. The typical 20-something employee is still trying to figure out everything for himself, and he's usually not as interested in mentoring you as older executives will be. In addition, people usually refer you "down" their network instead of "up" their network. In other words, people usually refer you to someone they feel is at or below their current career level. Most people won't feel comfortable introducing you to someone at a higher level than they are, and most people don't know many people above their current career level anyway. By aiming high, you get to speak to a person who has more people to refer you "down" to, and those people will have much more authority than the people a typical young professional could connect you with.

Here are five categories of Game-Changers that you should target through Cold Networking.

1.  *C-Level executives (the CEO, CFO, CMO, president, etc.).* Go to the top whenever you can. Just understand that it will be much harder to make contact with a C-Level executive at a larger organization (since there are more layers and gatekeepers to cut through). If an organization has fewer than 100 employees, you can often get right to the president or CEO without too many obstacles. If you approach her the right way, she will probably be impressed. The payoff is huge since you are talking to the head honcho. When I got my job after leaving the NBA in 2008, I had a strong relationship with the CEO of the next company that hired me. The result? He *created* a job for me. When targeting C-Level executives, don't overlook the importance of making favorable impressions on gatekeepers. Most people treat assistants and secretaries like societal outcasts, so you can stand out in a good way by showing them respect.

2.  *Senior-level sales, marketing, PR, or media executives.* These employees are usually the most visible, well-connected people in any organization or industry. They are usually friendly and personable since they make their salary based on an ability to build relationships. They tend to be very accessible given the nature of their work. It's worth looking for executives in these roles regardless of what you want to do because they probably know people in a variety of job functions.

3.  *Leaders of professional associations.* Regardless of where they work full-time, association leaders usually know everyone in

a given industry. Therefore, they know where "hidden jobs" are as well.

4. *Leaders of social media groups and communities.* Leaders of groups on LinkedIn or popular bloggers, for example, have huge influence in their industry. Some social media leaders have thousands of online connections or followers. Just understand that their visibility can make them popular targets for career advice.

5. *Industry freelancers and entrepreneurs.* Freelancers and entre-preneurs have to know a lot of people to survive, so they can be great networking contacts, especially if they used to work for an employer in an industry you want to break into. In addition, they probably don't have too many job-seekers hit-ting them up for career advice. Just be careful with this one. Many freelancers are actually unemployed and looking for full-time jobs themselves. You want to find people who are freelancers by choice.

## THE TWENTY-FIRST-CENTURY ICEBREAKER

Platforms like Twitter, LinkedIn, YouTube, WordPress, and Face-book are making it easier than ever before to connect with highly influential people in any industry or organization. Here are seven innovative, little-known secrets to how you can use social media to impress and connect with Game-Changers.

1. *Use LinkedIn group discussion archives to start conversations.* Once you join a group on LinkedIn, you have access to the archives of all prior discussions. This is very valuable because you can then search through all prior discussions based on keywords related to your career aspirations. Then, you can research and comment on prior discussions.

2. *Reply privately to LinkedIn group members.* When someone

posts a question or comments on a question inside a LinkedIn group discussion board, anyone else in the group can "reply privately" to that person. The "reply privately" button is not visible unless you move your mouse over someone's profile picture (which will be to the left of his or her comment), or if you move your mouse around underneath the comment.

3. *Ask great questions inside LinkedIn groups.* Just like at a networking event, asking an intelligent question on a group discussion board in LinkedIn is a great way to impress people and start conversations. You could post an article or link to a blog entry and ask members of the group for their opinions, or you could ask members to share their opinions on your own thought-provoking question. If you ask a great question inside a large LinkedIn group, you might get 25 to 50 responses or more. You can also just ask a question like one you would ask in an Advice Appointment (discussed a little later in this chapter). Just be sure to read through the group discussion archives first to make sure you are not asking a question that was asked by someone else recently. When people reply to your questions, you can receive an automatic message from LinkedIn. Then, you can "reply privately" as discussed above. (Caveat: Do not use questions as a way to promote yourself.)

4. *Use blog posts to start conversations.* You can write relevant articles on your own blog and/or you can comment on blogs by industry leaders. You can also use content from your blogs as material for the next secret.

5. *Use tweets to start conversations.* Take the links coming into your inbox from your Google alerts on your industry (you set up those alerts after reading Chapter 5, right?), and tweet links to those articles through your Twitter account. These tweets add value to your current/potential community and demonstrate your passion and/or expertise for a field. Don't expect people to find you because of your tweets, although it is possible. Just tweet to add value and so that people are impressed when they check you out.

6. *Use Facebook status updates to start conversations.* You can post the same links into your own Facebook status updates, and you can also post valuable comments on the Facebook pages you are following for your target employers and associations.

7. *Use YouTube videos to start conversations.* You can film your own videos connected to your field, or you can comment on videos posted by leaders in your industry.

As with any form of networking, your initial objective through Cold Networking with any social media platform is to get a conversation started with people in your ideal industry. The goal is not to promote yourself and your job search.

After you establish a dialogue, the next goal is to request an Advice Appointment. Meeting someone through Warm or Cool Networking is still superior to connecting with someone cold (via phone, email, or social media). However, social media sites provide phenomenal networking opportunities when in-person meetings are not feasible. Just be careful what you post online (especially if you are currently employed) and assume your Internet activity is visible to others (even if your privacy settings are strict).

## I SCHEDULED AN ADVICE APPOINTMENT! NOW WHAT???

Again, the goal of any form of networking is to get Advice Appointments with people working in the organizations or industry you want to break into. Here are six secrets for using these meetings to gather relevant information, job leads, and referrals.

### Treat Advice Appointments Like Job Interviews

Show up or call on time, and dress professionally if you are meeting in person. Chapter 7 will teach you everything you need to know about job interviews. For now, let's just say that you have to take Advice Appointments very seriously. (Bonus tip: Do whatever you can to meet the person *at his office*. You may get a chance to meet his colleagues as well.)

## Start the Right Way

Begin the Advice Appointment by making sure the time still works for the other person and by thanking her for meeting/speaking with you. Then, ask if you could share a quick 30-second background of yourself. It is important to offer a well-constructed bio at the start because you want the other person to understand why you requested the meeting and because it gives you a chance to highlight some of your strengths. Be concise and prepare this 30-second bio in advance; do not improvise this.

## Be Prepared to Lead

Unlike a traditional job interview where the interviewer takes the lead, you have to run the meeting in an Advice Appointment. An Advice Appointment will probably last only 15 to 30 minutes, so there is no way you will be able to ask more than five to 10 questions at the max. Don't waste the limited time you have with a senior executive to ask questions about a company's culture or someone's "typical day." You can get that information from other sources. When you are meeting with a heavy-hitter, your goal should be to impress the person and increase your chances of getting job leads and/or referrals. If you think that is manipulative, you need to chill out! You aren't forcing anyone to give you a job lead or referral against his will.

In general, here are the 10 best questions you can ask in an Advice Appointment. Just fill in the blanks based on your career goals and whom you are talking to:

1. How did you get started in _____, and what do you think has made you successful throughout your career?

2. What are some ways that other people you know have gotten started in _____?

3. What are the pros and cons of working in _____?

4. What traits, skills, or experiences does your organization/industry look for?

5. If you were me, what would you do to try to break into _____ now?

6. What publications, professional associations, or events should I check out for additional information on _____?

7. Do you know anyone else I can speak to for advice about breaking into _____?

8. Can you take a quick glance at my résumé and give me your feedback?

9. If I have additional questions in the future, can I reach out to you again?

10. How can I return the favor for your time?

## Be Respectful of the Other Person's Time

Stick to the amount of time you agreed to when setting up the Advice Appointment. The standard duration for a phone conversation is 15 minutes, and 20 to 30 minutes is typical for a face-to-face appointment.

## Thank the Other Person

Send a short thank-you note via email immediately after your conversation, while referencing any follow-up items or key takeaways from your discussion. You should also mail a handwritten thank-you note immediately after your conversation. (You may need to ask for a mailing address during the call/meeting.) Thank-you notes are imperative!

## Stay in Touch

The person meeting with you wants to see you succeed. By taking and implementing the advice someone has given you, you have shown that you valued her opinion and you have also made the person more invested in your eventual success.

# JOB SEARCH STRATEGY #4: APPLY AGGRESSIVELY FOR ADVERTISED JOBS

As I have hopefully drilled into your head by now, the best way to distinguish yourself during your job search is by leveraging personal contacts and relationships (i.e., Warm Networking, Cool Networking, and Cold Networking).

The next best way to stand out is through a strategy I call Applying Aggressively for advertised jobs. Jobs can be advertised through career pages on employer websites, on-campus recruiting at colleges, career fairs, online job boards, or newspapers. As I mentioned in Chapter 1, advertised jobs are usually a tease because they generally feature intense competition and lots of red-tape.

Do not waste your time pursuing advertised jobs *unless* you plan to Apply Aggressively. Most people do the opposite. They don't realize that the application process (like everything else during your job search) is a test and a way to stand out. In addition to the best-practice of customizing all your application materials based on the job you are applying for, here are five best-practices for when you apply for advertised jobs.

1. *Never apply for a job with an anonymous employer*. If you cannot see who the employer is, how you can be sure that it is

an organization you want to work for? How can you see if you have an "in" to the organization? How can you craft a personalized cover letter? How can you follow up? You can't! Therefore, it's not worth the time and energy of applying in the first place.

2. *Apply to a specific person.* Don't just apply to HR or "to whom it may concern," or be prepared for your application to end up in a black hole. Try to apply directly to the person you would report to if hired (or apply to that person's boss).

3. *Follow up on your application.* Make direct contact (ideally by phone) with the hiring person immediately after you apply. A short conversation or a brief voicemail with a 15- to 30-second pitch could provide the edge you need to land an interview. Some people will disagree with me, but I would still follow up even if the job advertisement specifically says not to follow up. Just say something like, "While I know you asked us not to follow up, I'm very excited about the opportunity to work for your organization, and I would love an opportunity to tell you why I believe I can deliver the results you are seeking better than anyone else." I would always rather have an employer think I was too bold than wonder to myself what might have happened if I had not been passive.

> LEIBMAN LIFE LESSON:
> *To get your dream job, you have to constantly ask yourself, "What else can I do to stand out in a good way from my competition?"*

4. *Add something extra.* Include something extra with your application, such as a relevant, impressive sample of your work.

5. *Get endorsed.* Include strategic endorsements during your application process somehow. You can do this by including letters of recommendation or by including a Recommendation Report (as discussed in Chapter 4). You could also have your best academic or professional advocates call the hiring

person on your behalf, or you can use the strategies from the rest of this chapter to see if you know anyone who currently works or previously worked for the employer. If so, make sure she provides an endorsement for you as well.

As shown through some of the success stories in this book, it is certainly possible to get your dream job by applying for an advertised job. However, it's worth noting that each of these people went above and beyond the "standard" application procedures. In other words, each person Applied Aggressively.

## JOB SEARCH Q&A WITH THE AUTHOR

Here are answers to some common questions from job-seekers as they look for jobs.

**Q:** What can I do to maintain a positive attitude while encountering rejection during my job search?

**A:** Rejection is inevitable during any job search, no matter how marketable and talented you are. Staying positive is very important. Surround yourself with optimistic people and fill your mind with inspirational books, CDs, tapes, and videos as much as possible. The optimism from these sources will rub off on you. The bottom line is that you need just one break, and it's closer than you think! Focus on what you can control: *your effort*. Your goal should be to talk to as many successful people as possible in your ideal industry. Each step you take gets you a little closer to your dream job. Keep going! It will be worth it.

**Q:** There is someone I want to reach out to for advice, but I don't have his contact information. Any ideas on how to track this guy down?

**A:** Start by visiting the website for the person's employer. Organizations with fewer than 100 employees often post full contact information online for their staff members. You can also Google the person and look him up on social media sites like LinkedIn and Twitter. If that doesn't work, you can also check out www.Jigsaw.com, a downloadable directory of contact information for millions of professionals worldwide. If you can't find the person in Jigsaw, just get the contact information for one of his colleagues, and extrapolate the email address. For example, let's say Paul Smith works for XYZ Company, and his email address is PaulSmith@XYZcompany.com. Then, the email address for nearly every other employee in the organization will be structured as FirstnameLastname@XYZcompany.com.

**Q:** What should I write when I email someone for career advice?

**A:** First of all, use a compelling subject line for your email (e.g., "Referral from Dave Jackson at ABC Company") and make sure your email is well-written and customized. Those efforts increase your chances of getting a quick, favorable response. You should personalize your email by highlighting a shared connection or affiliation or by referencing the person's work somehow. Then, share *your* dream with passion and confidence, so that the person knows you will not waste her time. (Remember *The Lemonade Stand Principle*.) Next, request an opportunity to ask the person for advice in person or through another channel. Do not ask for a job or for help finding a job. You can also include a high-value P.S., which could be another personalized question/comment or a link to an interesting, relevant article. Feel free to use the following example as a template that you can adjust:

> *Hi Mrs. Smith,*
>
> *Given your success and experience in the sports marketing industry, Dave Jackson at ABC Company suggested I send you an email.*
>
> *In May 2011, I will be graduating with Honors from Johns Hopkins University. I've worked extremely hard during my time at JHU and am willing to do whatever it takes to achieve my dream of landing a sales/marketing job with a pro sports franchise after college.*

*Would it be possible for us to schedule a 15- to 30-minute appointment for me to swing by your office or for us to speak on the phone? It would be great to meet you in person, learn more about how you got started in the field, and ask for some of your career advice. I know you are very busy, so thank you for your time and consideration, and please let me know what is most convenient for you.*

*P.S. Here is a link to an interesting article about the future of sports marketing that I thought you might enjoy: http://www. sampleinterestingarticle.com.*

> *Sincerely,*
> *Pete Leibman*
> *President of ABC Fraternity*
> *XYZ University, Class of 2012*
> *(333) 333-3333*
> *peteleibman@gmail.com*
> *www.linkedin.com/in/ peteleibman*

Note that in an e-mail, as opposed to a letter, you might want to put a P.S. above the signature so it doesn't get buried.

## Oliver Uberti Got His Dream Job with National Geographic *Magazine*

My mother still has the drawing of the Mayflower that I made in first grade. I always loved art but never thought I could make a living doing it. I eventually got an art scholarship to attend the University of Michigan, where I took classes in graphic design and scientific illustration. While studying abroad in New Zealand during my junior year, I spent a lot of time journaling about my interests. I drew a Venn diagram with three circles, one for each of the three elements I hoped my dream job would include: visual art, international issues, and a wide, global audience. When I looked at the spot where all three circles intersected, one organization stood out from the rest in meeting all my wishes: *National Geographic* magazine.

As I was getting set to graduate from college, *National Geographic* posted a job opening for an entry-level designer. I applied online, but I never heard back. Then, I sent the magazine a self-promotion package in the mail. I still did not hear back. I was leaving for Africa for five weeks on a scientific illustration trip soon, so I had to act quickly. The job would likely be filled by the time I got back. So, I packed up my car and drove back home to Philadelphia. I got my suit dry-cleaned, fixed up my portfolio, and then drove down to Washington, D.C., to go get my dream job. I had no interview scheduled. The way I looked at it, I was saving my future boss's time.

When I got to the *National Geographic* headquarters, I dialed the extension for the design director. When she answered, I immediately launched into my pitch. She said she was busy and that I should come back the following day at 3 p.m.

I stayed at my brother's house in Virginia that night. The next day, I put on the freshly dry-cleaned Brooks Brothers suit (which I had found at a thrift store in Michigan for $7) and I took the Metro to my interview. It was sweltering that afternoon, so I showed up to the interview "damp." Over a three- to four-hour period, I met with nearly everyone in the design department.

Many of the members of the design staff had heard about my upcoming trip to Africa and had asked to be on my list for email updates that I'd be writing from the field. As a result, the whole time that I was circling from South Africa to Botswana to Malawi and back down to South Africa, my voice was appearing in their inboxes while they interviewed other candidates.

During my trip, we traveled into Mozambique, where I was unforeseeably out of email contact for nine days. When we entered Swaziland, I rushed right to an Internet cafe, where I found a slew of emails waiting for me from the design director. They were offering me the job, which I immediately accepted.

I got my dream job and so can you!

—OLIVER UBERTI

CHAPTER 7

# EXECUTE

## (STEP #6)

> "Whoever said, 'It's not whether you win or lose that counts,' probably lost."
>
> —MARTINA NAVRATILOVA, WINNER OF 20 WIMBLEDON TITLES

2:58 p.m., May 27, 2003: at the offices of the Washington Wizards (in the main lobby)

My heart was beating so fast and so hard that I thought it might pop out of my chest.

Even worse, my hands were dripping in sweat.

All I could think was, *"Ms. O'Malley is going to freak out when I shake her hand because I'm gonna give her a bath."*

In a desperate attempt to keep my hand dry, I was actually seated there with my right hand underneath my right leg, trying to wipe the sweat off my palm.

This was it. It was crunch-time. In two minutes, I was going to walk into a job interview with the team president of the Washington Wizards. As I sat in the lobby outside her office, I tried to control my nerves.

Moments later, Susan O'Malley emerged, and in her very professional tone, she said, "Peter, come with me." I looked at her, and to this day, it's the only time I have ever been terrified by the sight of a woman who weighed about 100 pounds.

However, this was different from the last time the team interviewed me. Unlike one year earlier, when the team interviewed me for an internship position, this time I was extremely well-prepared.

We met for 30 to 40 minutes, and at the end of the interview, I looked her right in the eyes and said, "Ms. O'Malley, I want this very badly. I promise that if you give me a chance, you will not regret it."

She looked me back in the eyes and said, "Pete, I love your conviction. You would be amazed how rarely people tell me they want the job."

> **LEIBMAN LIFE LESSON:**
>
> *It is not "impossible to get your dream job" with little or no industry experience.*

One week later, my dream became a reality when the Wizards offered me a full-time position in their front office.

The #1 objective of this chapter is to walk you through the do's, don'ts, and secrets for success in the interview process. More specifically, you will learn the following:

- ► How to avoid the biggest interview sins

- ► How to prepare for any job interview so that you can walk in with confidence

- ► How to answer the most common interview questions

- ► How to impress the interviewer by selling yourself without bragging

- ► How to transition from the interview to a job offer

## SIX DEADLY INTERVIEWING SINS

Here are the six biggest sins committed by job-seekers during interviews. Watch out for them!

1. *You don't bring your "A" game throughout the entire process.* The job is won or lost before the interview begins, based on your preparation. The interview process begins the moment you come in contact with someone who could potentially refer you or hire you. Treat every career conversation like an interview, because every career conversation *is* an interview. You want each person you meet (including secretaries) to be sold on hiring you because you never know who has the final say. It takes only one person adamant against hiring you for you to lose a job offer.

2. *You have not taken the steps necessary to control your anxiety.* It's normal to be nervous in a job interview! You can control and reduce your anxiety by being well-prepared, practicing ahead of time, looking your best, showing up early, and so on. You don't have to be perfect, so try to relax.

3. *You are not professional at all times.* I won't list all the possible ways you could be unprofessional. Let's just say that you can blow your chances of getting hired in the first three seconds you meet someone. Make sure you have confident body language, your breath is fresh, and you don't have any body odor or smell like cigarette smoke. Make sure you are nicely groomed. Turn your cell phone off before the interview. Don't say anything that could damage your chances. Don't volunteer more information than is needed. Never let your guard down. And . . . don't be weird! Seriously. One of my friends started her own business recently, and she told me of all sorts of bizarre ways that people showed up and acted in interviews. She said it was amazing how hard it was to find someone who was "normal."

4. *You give the interviewer too much credit.* Do not make the person interviewing you into some almighty king or queen. When I interviewed as a college student with Susan O'Malley— an NBA team president— I talked to her like an equal, and she respected me for that. Do not assume the interviewer is an expert at interviewing/hiring. I conducted interviews for a

previous employer and I had no formal training, and none of my colleagues did either. This happens more often than you might think and more often than any employer will publicly admit. Also, do not assume the interviewer is familiar with your background. I once interviewed with a senior executive when I was in the process of leaving my job in the NBA. I showed up with a professional portfolio with the Wizards logo on it. The interviewer said, "Oh, are you a big Wizards fan or something?" I replied, "Well, yes, I work for the team." He said, "Oh, wow, that must be very cool." The guy had clearly not even read my résumé or cover letter. Again, this happens more often than you might think. The person interviewing you probably has a lot of other responsibilities on her plate, so she might not always get a chance to review your application materials before meeting you.

5.  *You do not know how to sell yourself.* Don't assume credentials will speak for themselves. It is your responsibility to prove to the employer why you are the best person for the job. Selling yourself is not bragging about how great you are. The best ways to sell yourself are by being professional, asking great questions, sharing stories and examples that demonstrate why you have the traits and skills needed for success in the position, and closing the interview strong. You can finish strong by asking for the job while recapping why you are the best candidate.

6.  *You are not perceived as likable.* Another reason why interviews exist is because employers hire people they like. The most qualified candidate is not always the person who gets the job. Just like with networking, the goal during the *entire* interview process is to present yourself as someone who is genuine, enthusiastic, friendly, and professional. Treat every person with respect. If you are rude to the secretary, you are not going to get hired. Don't badmouth anyone or be negative. Also, don't be a robot; include humor when appropriate. If you have to fake enthusiasm, that's a sign you should *not* be interviewing with the organization. If you can't get excited

for one hour about the possibility of working for the employer, do you really think you will be excited working for the organization 40 to 50 hours a week? While there will always be people who won't like you for reasons beyond your control, great body language and a positive attitude will significantly increase your chances of being perceived as likable.

## YOU'D BETTER DO YOUR HOMEWORK

While an interview is not a test, you should prepare for it as if it is. Do your homework before you arrive, and you will be much more confident and impressive in your presentation. Here are three preparation secrets to know before every job interview.

### Research the Person or People Interviewing You

Google them, look them up on social media sites like LinkedIn, Facebook, and Twitter, and read their profiles (if provided on the employer's website). If they have a blog or have written other articles, definitely read through that or them as well. Ultimately, you want to gain a better understanding of their personal and professional background, so that you can build genuine rapport and establish commonality during the interview process. You want to know where they went to school, how they got started with their current employer, how long they have been there, where else they have worked, what their personal interests are, and if you have any shared affiliations or connections with them. Most people will be flattered that you took the time to do this, so don't be shy about mentioning that you looked them up before meeting them.

### Research the Employer and the Industry

Read through the employer's website, Google the employer, check out its social media pages, and read through the Insider Information you should be receiving (as discussed in Chapter 5). You should also visit www.glassdoor.com, where you can often find insights from people who have interviewed with specific employers. The process of researching the employer and the industry should actually be interesting to you. If not, that's a sign that you are interviewing with the wrong employer or that you don't want the job badly enough.

## Identify the Employer's Specific Needs

Study the job description and the employer's website meticulously. This sounds incredibly obvious, but most people take this for granted. I certainly did before some of my first job interviews. The job description and employer's website usually tip you off to what you will be asked in the interview, while also giving you ideas for great questions you should ask. Here are three powerful questions to ask yourself to identify the employer's needs:

1. *What results is the employer looking for from the person who will be hired for this position?*

2. *What skills seem to be most essential for success with this organization and in the position I am applying for?*

3. *What personality traits seem to be most essential for success with this organization and in the position I am applying for?*

# BE PARANOID

Before you try to sell a product, you always need to identify your prospect's likely objections or concerns about buying. The same is true when trying to get hired. Then, once you have identified the objections, you prepare ways to overcome those objections before they surface (most objections are never shared), and you also prepare how to respond if the prospect challenges you with a question you would rather not answer. This might sound paranoid, but it's worth the effort. It takes only one tough question to throw you off your game.

While interviewing with a Fortune 100 company as a student in college, I was concerned that the people there might ask me where else I was interviewing. At the time, I did not have any other interviews scheduled. However, rather than facing my fear during my preparation for the interview and developing an appropriate answer, I simply hoped it would not come up.

> **LEIBMAN LIFE LESSON:**
> *Anticipate possible objections before the interview. You don't want to improvise your comeback when the pressure is on.*

Unfortunately, they asked. When I tried to create an impromptu answer, I ultimately sounded like I was trying to lie. It was a disaster.

Everyone has insecurities during a job search as to why someone might not think he should be hired. You might be worried about your major (even though it doesn't matter), or your GPA, or your lack of work experience, or the fact that you have been unemployed for five months, or something else. Rather than hoping it doesn't come up in the interview process, why not address it before the interview? Ask yourself these three questions:

1. *If I was the employer, why would I not hire me?*

2. *What could an employer ask me in an interview that would make me squirm?*

3. *What could an employer ask me to do in the interview to prove I can handle the job I am applying for?* For example, if you are interviewing for a sales job, you better be prepared to discuss how you would sell one of the employer's products or services.

Walking into an interview prepared to overcome any objection or concern is one of the best ways to be confident and perform your best.

*Five Secrets for Acing Any Interview Question*

1. *Maintain positive body language.* How you answer is usually more important than what you say.

2. *Maintain positive verbal language.* Never speak negatively about yourself or another person or organization. Employers hire people with positive, winning attitudes.

3. *Be concise.* When in doubt, answer any question in 30 to 60 seconds. Then say, "I can elaborate if you would like," or ask the employer a relevant question in response to the one you were just asked. Interviews should feel like conversations, not interviews.

4. *Focus on results.* Employers view past performance as a predictor of future performance. Make sure to emphasize the positive impact of your prior experiences.

5. *Stay focused.* Everything you say must be presented in a way that is relevant to the employer's needs and the job you are applying for. If you are ever unclear on an employer's question, ask for clarification before answering. Do not go off on tangents.

## ANTICIPATE LIKELY QUESTIONS

When I speak to large groups in public, I always take group Q&A after my presentations. Some speakers don't like to do this because you can't be certain what the audience might ask you. In a way, it's kind of like conducting a job interview in front of several hundred people or more.

So, how do I prepare for this? Well, I certainly don't practice answering 100 to 200 or more possible questions. Instead, I just ask myself what I'm likely to be asked, given the audience and my topic. Without fail, I can break down the possible questions into five to 10 primary categories. Then, I just practice answering one question representative of each of those main categories. This approach has served me well and saved me hours of prep time.

While I appreciate the detail that some other authors have gone through in compiling tips on how to answer 100 to 200 "common" interview questions, it's a poor use of time and energy to prepare answers for so many different questions. I certainly didn't do that during any of my successful job searches. (However, if you actually want to practice answering 100 to 200 interview questions, just Google the phrase "interview questions.")

In general, employers are ultimately trying to answer two questions: "Why us?" and "Why you?" In other words, they want to know why you want the job and why they should hire you.

To anticipate what you will be asked in your job interview, ask yourself these questions:

► *If the roles were reversed and I was conducting the interview, what would I be asking?*

► *If I had to interview someone for this position based on the job description, what would I ask?*

By putting yourself in the employer's shoes temporarily, you can usually identify the main questions you will be asked. Then, you just have to prepare your answers. More specifically, there are only seven categories of interview questions.

## Category #1: Your Background

*How to answer:* Whenever an interviewer asks a question about your background (e.g., how you selected your major, how you selected your college), always tie your answer back to why you want the job and why the employer should hire you.

## Category #2: Your Goals

*How to answer:* Be specific about what appeals to you about working for the employer and what excites you about the specific position you are interviewing for. Then, provide some evidence on why you believe you would succeed in the position and how you can further support the employer's mission. By going through the self-assessment questions from Chapter 3, you should be able to answer any questions about your goals with ease.

## Category #3: Your Strengths and Accomplishments

*How to answer:* Discuss strengths that are most relevant to the job you are applying for, and discuss how those strengths led to prior achievements. Ideally, you want to share examples regarding how you delivered results similar to the results the employer is seeking in your position.

## Category #4: Your Weaknesses and Dislikes

*How to answer:* Employers ask questions in this category to see if you will give them a reason to remove you from consideration. Don't take the bait when an interviewer asks you about something negative! Instead, stay positive and professional, never bad-mouth any person or other organization, and stay focused on your strengths. Make sure you are especially concise when answering questions in this category. Do not ramble—this could be dangerous.

Humor (especially self-deprecating humor) can be very effective when someone asks any question about why you should not be hired. Humor breaks the ice and shows you can stay relaxed under pressure. Just keep it professional, and don't try too hard. For example, if someone asked me in an interview what my greatest weakness was, I would smile and pause, and then I would say, "Well, my jump-shot is not what it used to be." Then, I would highlight a weakness not connected to the skill set or knowledge base needed for success in the job I was applying for.

## Category #5: Your People/Communication Skills

*How to answer:* Emphasize interpersonal traits that are positive and relevant to the position you are applying for, and offer to give a quick example/story that proves you have each of those traits.

## Category #6: Your Character

*How to answer:* The employer wants to see that you can handle challenges. Share a story that talks about how you overcame an obstacle to achieve a desirable result. It's even better if the result you achieved is highly relevant to the position you are applying for. For example, if you are applying for a teaching job, you could talk about dealing with a difficult student in a prior role.

## Category #7: Your Salary

*How to answer:* When asked about your current salary or future salary needs, emphasize that you prefer to look at the entire compensation package, including professional development opportunities and growth potential. (That should be the truth.) Then, say you are confident that a fair compensation package can be arranged if you both agree there is a fit. The best time to discuss salary is after you have shown the tremendous value you could deliver and after you have received an offer. Never throw out a number first.

## HOW CAN I SELL MYSELF WITHOUT BRAGGING?

Selling yourself is not when you robotically recite your achievements or tell the interviewer how great you are. Here are six ways to sell yourself effectively (i.e., without bragging).

## 1. Strategic Success Stories

Strategic success stories are among your best sales tools as a job-seeker because they prove that you are the right type of person. When an employer says, "Tell me about a time when _____," the employer is asking you to tell a story.

Yes, you have stories. Everyone has stories! I had a student come up to me after a presentation in 2011 and tell me she didn't have any stories, even though she had moved to the United States from Nigeria as a teenager. She was surprised to learn that this experience was an appropriate topic to discuss in an interview. Here's the bottom line. Stories don't have to come just from time spent in an office. Stories from your personal life can be very powerful (e.g., stories from collegiate sports teams, class projects, volunteer opportunities, extracurricular activities, travel/study abroad programs). Just use good judgment.

A strategic success story should include a *problem*, the *actions* you took, and the positive *results* you achieved (*PAR*). Be prepared to tell at least one story that proves you have each of the personality traits and skill sets you identified earlier in this chapter through your employer research. Again, you can usually predict which stories you will be asked to share or which stories you should volunteer on your own by reading the job description and employer's website (especially where the employer shares its mission statement or core values). In addition, you should have each of the following five types of stories in your arsenal for every job interview.

1. *A "defining moment."* While you probably have several "defining moment" stories (trust me, you have them), you want to prepare one that is relevant to the job you are applying for. For example, when I interviewed with the Wizards, I told the story of my father taking me to my first NBA game when I was seven years old and how I decided that night that I wanted to work in the NBA when I was older. A "defining moment" story that is well-constructed and highly relevant will make the hiring person believe that you are "destined" for the position. It also minimizes the employer's concern that you will bolt for another job after getting hired. It gets the hiring per-

son to think, "Wow, we have to hire this person. This person was born to work here. This person will be committed."

2. *Leadership/initiative*. Every employer wants to hire people who are proactive. Think of one to two examples of times when you led or created something that was successful.

3. *Problem solving*. Employers want people who can solve problems and who will embrace challenges and hard work. Think of one to two times when you overcame a problem or obstacle in your life.

> LEIBMAN LIFE LESSON:
> *Strategic success stories sell. Make sure you have five to 10 in your pocket for every interview.*

4. *Teamwork*. Getting along well with others is imperative for workplace success. Think of one to two times when you worked as part of a team to achieve desirable results.

5. *Creativity*. Creativity is essential for growth in any organization. Think of one to two times when you did something innovative.

## 2. The Smart Start

After some initial small talk, nearly every interview begins with the interviewer saying, "So, tell me about yourself." The way you respond to this seemingly innocent comment lays the foundation for the rest of the interview. You do not want to improvise your response. Be prepared to share a 30- to 60-second answer that highlights your relevant background, why you want the job, and why the organization should hire you. Write this out in advance so that you can practice it. Getting off to a strong start in the interview will give you confidence and solidify a great first impression. Some words of caution: Make sure not to sound like a robot when answering this (you should be able to talk about yourself naturally!), do not lay it on too thick here, and do not speak for more than 60 seconds.

## 3. The Killer Close

This is your final pitch at the end of the interview. While this will need to be adjusted on the spot based on what is discussed in the interview itself, you should prepare an outline before the interview. This is way too important to improvise completely. Like "The Smart Start," you want to discuss why you want the job and why the organization should hire you. You also want to overcome any objections the interviewer could have about hiring you, and you want to ask for the job.

> **LEIBMAN LIFE LESSON:**
> *Your first words and last words in an interview will be the most memorable. Craft them with care by using the tips in "The Smart Start" and "The Killer Close."*

## 4. Unsolicited Endorsements

As discussed in Chapter 4, the best way to brag is to get someone else to brag for you. It does not matter if the interviewer requested references. In fact, it is better if the interviewer did not request them because that means most people will not bring them, allowing you to stand out in one more way.

Here is a bonus tip. Get one to two of your references to call the hiring person *before* your interview. Credit for this idea goes to my father. He is a former school principal, and he is currently professor of education for St. Francis College in New York. He actually makes unsolicited calls to hiring persons before his students' interviews. His endorsement carries a lot of weight since he used to be a school principal, so he can speak the language of the interviewers and address their concerns and hot buttons. The result? His success rate in getting his students placed is through the roof because he sells the candidates before they ever get to the interview.

Hiring persons are always impressed that a candidate's professor was willing to call on his behalf.

## 5. The Risk-Remover

As discussed in Chapter 1, employers have lots of fears about hiring the wrong person. A great way to prove you are low-risk is to bring a relevant work sample and/or action plan to your interview. Most people barely even check out the company website before going on an interview, so if you do this, you will leapfrog over your competition. In terms of what to bring or create, it obviously depends on the job you are applying for. However, here are some ideas:

- A copy of a publication that featured an article you wrote

- A copy of several articles you posted on a blog

- A DVD featuring footage of a website you designed

- A summary of a class project where you designed a marketing plan for a local business

- A summary of what you have done to become an industry expert (e.g., joining relevant associations, reading relevant books, subscribing to publications)

- A list of ideas on what you would do to deliver results in the first 30 to 60 days on the job

Again, you want to remove any possible concerns an employer might have about your commitment and enthusiasm, and you want to prove that you are more than capable of delivering the results needed. Even if you provide just a few ideas on one page, this will really make you stand out. As with anything, just make sure to be professional and make sure whatever you bring is relevant to the job you are applying for.

## 6. Customized Questions

An interview is like a first date: Regardless of who sets it up, it is designed for each party to decide if there is a match. Another one of the ways I stood out during the interview process with the Washington Wizards was by asking intelligent questions. For example, the team had just removed Michael Jordan from his management position with the team, so I asked about the reaction from the fan base and how the team was moving forward despite those PR challenges. I also asked about a policy I had read about online in which the team decided to refund season ticket holders who were unhappy about the decision to remove MJ. These questions were not that challenging to brainstorm in advance, and they definitely showed that I was tuned in. Susan O'Malley commented at one point that my interview was "the toughest interview she had experienced in a while." She was obviously kidding, but her comment showed that I had surely impressed her.

The goal here is not to stump the interviewer or to put her on the hot seat. However, you want to show your interest in the organization and the position. You also get to decide if the position is a fit for you. Perhaps most important, the answers provided by the interviewer will help you craft your "Killer Close" at the end of the interview (a sales secret). Here are 10 of my favorite questions to *ask* in an interview:

1. How did you get to where you are today, and what do you think has made you successful?

2. What types of people do really well with this organization?

3. Where does this organization want to be in five to 10 years?

4. How will performance be measured for this position, and what career paths are available for people who succeed in this position?

5. How did this position become available?

6. What do you believe is the greatest threat to the future success of the department/organization/industry?

7. What impact do you believe _____ [insert recent trend, policy, event, etc.] will have on the future of the department/organization/industry?

8. How has the department/organization/industry changed since _____ [insert recent trend, policy, event, etc.] or since _____ [insert when the interviewer started working there]?

9. Now that you have gotten to know a little more about me, what concerns, if any, would you have about hiring me for this position? (Consider asking this toward the end of the interview.)

10. What are the next steps in the interview process? (Get permission to follow up within a certain timeframe if no specific follow-up step is highlighted.)

By preparing great questions in advance (including more customized questions not listed above) and by asking them throughout the interview (and not just at the end of the interview), you can turn the interview into a two-way conversation. Since these questions show that you are evaluating the employer, there is also a clear message that you are not desperate, which makes you even more desirable.

> LEIBMAN LIFE LESSON:
> *The best way to demonstrate your intelligence and enthusiasm is to ask great questions.*

## THE INTERVIEW IS OVER!

Time to relax, right?

Wrong. Here are six secrets to get from job interview to job offer.

## 1. Debrief

Immediately after the interview ends, go somewhere quiet to gather your thoughts. Write down every question you can remember being asked, along with anything you learned about the interviewer, the employer, or the industry. This will be especially valuable if you are called in for another interview or if you interview with another employer in that industry. You should also take note of what you think you could do better next time, and you should make a list of any follow-up items.

## 2. Say Thank You Twice

First, send a personalized email to thank every single person you met during your interview. This message should be sent within a few hours of the interview ending. Then, depending on the timeline for next steps, you should also send a handwritten (or typed) thank-you note to each person you met. Make sure each letter includes some sort of personal comment about your interaction, and if you send both an email and a letter, make sure each communication is different. You can also use a thank-you note to reiterate why you want the job and why you should be hired or to follow up on anything you wish you had mentioned or done differently. As with all written communications, make sure you write professionally, and proofread before sending.

## 3. Get Endorsed

If you have not had your references contact the hiring person on your behalf, make sure you have them do so after the interview. Again, this is just one more way to stand out from other candidates, who will likely just wait to be asked for references.

## 4. Consider the Entire Package During the Salary Negotiation Process

While base/starting salary is a significant factor, most people ignore the other components of a compensation package. These include growth potential, performance-based incentives (i.e., commission and bonuses), your title, your office space/location/environment, flexibility in your hours, insurance coverage, 401k/financial packages, vacation/sick days, and expense accounts. Throughout my career, I have negotiated new titles, my own private office, more vacation/sick days, and a variety of other perks. (Full disclosure: These extra perks were negotiated during my tenure in the NBA and when I looked for a job after I left the NBA in 2008. I did not attempt to negotiate at all with my first job in the NBA right out of college.)

There is a lot of room for creativity with salary negotiation. If an employer is not willing to raise your pay, it may be very agreeable to other forms of compensation that could have even more value to you. When evaluating offers, don't forget about other nontangible benefits, such as the personal enjoyment you will derive from the job, the caliber of the boss you will work for (very important), and how much interest the employer has in you for its long-term plans. Negotiating power is all about leverage and how badly the employer wants you. The more the employer wants you, the more leverage you have. The salary negotiation process is *very* personalized based on your specific situation and based on the employer.

## 5. Evaluate Offers Carefully

You should get a minimum of one to two days to evaluate any offer, and all offers should be provided in writing. If the organization is not willing to grant you some time to think it over, it doesn't want you badly enough, and that's a major red flag. Having said that, be aware that you should never make threats, pit employers/offers against each other, or make unreasonable demands. Job offers can be taken off the table, and bridges can be burned for good. While you should always try to get what you are worth (or a little more!), never jeopardize an offer or a professional relationship to make a little more money.

## 6. Play Until the Final Whistle

No matter how well any interview goes, keep your job search alive until you actually start working for your next employer. Never abandon your job search because you think a job offer is imminent. Unfortunately, things can change.

## JOB SEARCH Q&A WITH THE AUTHOR

Here are answers to some common questions from job-seekers about interviews.

**Q:** What should I do in the 24 hours leading up to a job interview?

**A:** Here are some tips *for the night before* an interview:

► *Check the weather forecast for the day of your interview.* If it rains (and you show up wet) or if it is going to be 100 degrees (and you show up sweaty), you'll feel self-conscious and look bad.

► *Plan your travel.* Determine your mode of transportation (e.g., bus, train, car), map out your route to the interview location, and calculate how long it should take you to get there. Leave yourself at least two to three times as long as you think you will need. I once interviewed for a job in Washington, D.C., while I was a student in Baltimore. Having never been to the employer's office, I underestimated how long it would take to get there, and I showed up 40 minutes late. The interviewers were not impressed. Lateness is always inexcusable.

► *Get your clothes ready*. Make sure you will look like a "10" for your interview. This is not just to impress the people interviewing you—it's to make you feel great about yourself as well.

► *Gather everything you need to bring to the interview*. This includes a photo ID, copies of your résumé printed on high-quality paper, endorsements (even if they were not requested), a typed page with questions you plan to ask at the interview, any relevant research or notes you gathered on the employer/person interviewing you, and any other materials that have been requested by the interviewer or that you plan to bring as additional support for your candidacy.

► *Get a good night's rest.*

Here are some tips *for the day of* the interview:

► *Take care of your body*. Get in a workout at the gym as close to the interview as possible, while still leaving yourself plenty of time to shower and arrive early. Exercise will jump-start your energy levels and release stress. Be sure to eat smart throughout the day as well. You don't want to be starving during the interview, and you don't want to be digesting a Chipotle burrito either.

► *Travel in comfort*. In other words, if it's going to be 100 degrees, don't wear your entire suit to the interview. If you are driving to the interview, if possible, dress comfortably and then change at a nearby location.

► *Arrive early*. Arrive 30 to 60 minutes early, and make sure you know exactly where you need to go—but do *not* show up for the interview that early. Instead, go somewhere quiet nearby where you can focus and relax. You should actually show up for your interview five to 10 minutes early. Be friendly to everyone you meet inside, and assume you are being watched from the moment you enter the building (or parking lot). Pretend each person you meet could be the decision-maker on your getting the job. Many organizations get feedback from secretaries on people they are interviewing.

**Q:** I get really nervous during job interviews. What can I do to control my anxiety?

**A:** First, remember that everyone gets nervous during job interviews. You should remember that you are also interviewing the employer and that you have other options. Don't put too much pressure on yourself. Employers don't expect you to be perfect. Preparation and practice will make you less nervous once the interview gets under way. You can practice ahead of time with a stopwatch to make sure you are answering questions and telling stories within about 60 seconds. You can practice in front of the mirror (yes, this will feel very awkward at first!) to make sure your body language is confident and friendly. You can practice on tape by recording yourself (with audio or video) and then reviewing the footage for ideas on how to improve. You should also do mock interviews with someone you trust (e.g., a friend, family member, or career coach). In summary, interviewing is like anything: It gets easier with practice.

**Q:** I have an interview scheduled during a meal. What do I need to keep in mind?

**A:** Here are three tips:

- ► *Treat it with the same care as a traditional interview.* Never let your guard down. Regardless of where an interview takes place, it's still an interview.

- ► *Eat carefully.* Order something that will be easy to eat and not sloppy (think grilled chicken and rice rather than buffalo wings or spaghetti). Do not drink any alcohol.

▶ *Be ready for more chit-chat.* Be prepared to make more small talk than you would in a traditional interview.

**Q:** They want to do a phone/Skype interview with me. What do I need to keep in mind?

**A:** Here are a few tips for telephone interviews:

▶ *Take it seriously.* Employers often use a telephone interview as a preliminary screening tool. If you approach a phone interview too casually, you will never make it to a live interview.

▶ *Focus.* Make or take the call from a landline or from a location where you get clear cell phone service. Eliminate any potential distractions: Put your dog away, turn off your TV, and make/take the call in a quiet place. You should also have your résumé, list of questions to ask, and other notes in front of you.

▶ *Monitor your body language carefully.* Your body language will "come through" over the phone, so make sure you smile often, minimize fidgeting, and sit up straight (or stand up). You should also dress professionally for telephone interviews. While the interviewer will not be able to see if you are wearing pajamas, you'll project yourself much more confidently if you look your best.

▶ *Speak carefully.* Enunciate clearly and minimize filler words like "um" and "ah." Filler words are much more noticeable in telephone interviews than during in-person interviews.

Note that the same rules apply for Skype. Employers often use Skype interviews the same way they use telephone interviews, for preliminary screening. Just pay extra attention to the environment you will be taking/making the call from since it will be visible. Also, test your system ahead of time to avoid technical difficulties.

**Q:** I got a huge cut on my face that looks like I was in a bar fight. My interview is tomorrow. What should I do?!

**A:** In 2009, I went on an appointment with a business partner who showed up for the meeting with a huge black eye. (Apparently, it is not a good idea to stand behind your 10-year-old son while teaching him how to swing a golf club.) My colleague looked like he had been in a UFC match, which was not the impression we wanted to give to a potential client we were meeting for the first time. However, the way my colleague handled the situation was perfect. Within seconds of meeting our prospects, he joked about his eye by saying that he would never teach his 10-year-old how to play golf ever again. The prospects cracked up, the ice was broken, and he prevented them from wondering for the next hour what the heck he did to himself. If you have some sort of temporary injury or issue, acknowledge it early. You don't need to say anything if you have a prosthetic leg or a huge pimple on your forehead (hey, zit happens), but you should address anything that could cause someone to think negatively of your character.

**Q:** How should I respond if an employer asks me a strange question?

**A:** If an interviewer is not friendly or if she asks you an oddball question, don't take it personally. She is probably just testing your mettle. My brother, Matt, was once asked the following in an interview: "If I told you to prepare 50 BLTs, how would you do it?" Since he was interviewing for a corporate sales job (and not a position at McDonald's), he was understandably caught off-guard.

If you are asked how to do something strange, remain calm. Then, find a way to work in some light humor while asking the interviewer a series of your own questions. For example, if I had been asked how to make 50 BLTs, I would have flashed a smile and responded with something like, "Hmmm. . . . Well, would you like fries and shakes with that?" Then, I would have asked the following questions before coming up with my answer:

► What type of resources (i.e., help or equipment) do I have to make the BLTs?

► Who am I making the BLTs for?

► When do you need the BLTs to be finished?

► How will my performance be evaluated on this task?

When presented with a weird interview question, work in some light humor and be calm, confident, and curious.

## Erick van Zanten Got His Dream Job with General Electric

I am now a member of the Information Management Leadership Program (IMLP) at General Electric (GE). It is a very competitive program designed to train the future information management leadership in the company.

The traditional path to enter this program is to do well in one or more IMLP internships and graduate from a university where GE actively recruits with a degree in management information systems. I did not attend one of these universities, my only internship was not in any way related to IMLP, and my education was in engineering. I was nowhere near this typical path; I was the newcomer, and I was competing against people who already had IMLP experience and whose education more closely matched the traditional program member. The only chance I had was to impress my interviewers during my interviews and presentations.

In preparing for the interview, I asked my father for advice, and he replied with: "When you have many years of work, you are hired mainly because of experience. When you are fresh out of college, you are hired because of your character and potential." I took this advice to heart and prepared my presentation not to showcase how there might be some overlap between me and the archetypical member of the IMLP, but to show how my experiences in other fields had developed my character and how GE could benefit from hiring me.

I drew from experiences that I thought had nothing to do with me being admitted into an information management leadership training program. I talked about my involvement with triathlons and marathons to show that I was determined, disciplined, and hard-working. I talked about teaching myself iPhone programming to show my initiative and self-motivation. I talked about my leadership in clubs in college to demonstrate my leadership ability. I also sent each and every one of my interviewers a personalized thank-you note.

In the end, the combination of my presentation, my follow-up, and a very good review from my previous internship was enough to ensure that I received an offer to join the GE IMLP program.

I got my dream job and so can you!

—ERICK VAN ZANTEN

# PART II

# SKYROCKET YOUR CAREER WITH STEP #7 (B.E.P.R.O.)

# BELIEF

## (SUCCESS SECRET #1)

> "To be a champ, you have to believe in yourself when nobody else will."
>
> —SUGAR RAY LEONARD, OLYMPIC GOLD MEDALIST AND FORMER WBC
> WELTERWEIGHT BOXING CHAMPION

February 11, 1999: at Garden City High School (on our practice court)

All I could think to myself was, *"This is our reward for going 12–0 in the division?"*

After I had led my high school basketball team to only its third undefeated season in more than 50 years, my coach had just informed the team that we somehow got passed over for the #1 seed and instead received the #2 seed in the Nassau County playoffs. Our opponent?

Perennial powerhouse Westbury High School.

At the start of the season, Westbury High School had (as always) been seeded #1 out of the 12 teams in our division, while my team had (as always) been seeded toward the bottom (#7 that year).

However, we had a magical run that included a huge win over Westbury on its court several weeks earlier. I lived up to my "Pistol Pete" nickname that night, scoring 17 points in the first half alone and having the game-winning assist late in the fourth quarter. Westbury, on the other hand, struggled uncharacteristically all year long, barely eking its way into the county playoffs as a #15 seed.

In hindsight, my confidence should have been sky-high going into that playoff game. I had just been recognized as a First-Team All-County basketball player, we had won 12 games in a row, we had beaten Westbury on its own court, and now we got to play that team at home.

However, all I did was worry. I spent the next week focused on everything that could go wrong, and my fears became reality. I lost that game before I ever walked on the court. Westbury beat us in that playoff game by 11 points, as I played one of the worst basketball games of my life. It was a devastating end to an otherwise amazing season and high school career.

My basketball career never recovered after that painful defeat. The following year, I started my college basketball career at Johns Hopkins University. I really struggled with the transition when I got to college. It was the first time I had been away from home for more than four days in a row, and it was hard for me to adjust to that significant life change, while also trying to find my way in a much more competitive athletic environment.

Instead of being one of the taller, stronger guys, as I was on my high school team, I was suddenly smaller and weaker than everyone around me. Combine that with a hangover from my last high school game, a serious case of self-doubt, and a college coach who didn't seem to care about my development, and my confidence on the court evaporated. Rather than getting more comfortable as the year progressed, I allowed my fear to spiral out of control and overwhelm me. This resulted in mental and physical errors on the court I had never made before, which led to public and private criticism from my coach, which led to even lower confidence.

> **LEIBMAN LIFE LESSON:**
> *Believing you can succeed won't guarantee that you will (you still need to take the right actions), but believing you can't succeed will guarantee that you won't.*
> *Believe in yourself!*

Mentally drained and defeated, I quit the team the next year.

When reflecting on my life, I have noticed one common theme

between my successes and "failures." Without exception, I have succeeded when I have been willing to do whatever it takes and when I have believed that success was possible. Fear was present during both my successes *and* failures; the way I responded to fear was what determined the outcome.

Think back to some of your greatest successes and failures. I'd be willing to bet your belief (or lack of belief) impacted the outcome.

Fear and self-doubt will creep in any time you start a new job or career or when you step out of your comfort zone somehow at work or in your personal life. Understand that it's normal. It's part of being human! How you *respond* to that fear is what matters.

## SUCCESS BEGINS IN YOUR HEAD

The most important relationship in your career (and your life) is the relationship you have with yourself. While some people will consider that statement corny, it's 100 percent true.

The way you see yourself will impact your actions, your performance, and the relationships you have with others. If you don't believe in yourself, you will sabotage yourself in ways you won't even realize, you will quit too soon (or never try to begin with), and you will never come anywhere close to your full potential. It will also be impossible for you to get along well with other people (personally, romantically, and professionally).

There are three great myths about confidence:

1. *Myth #1: Confidence is inborn.* (No, it's developed.)

2. *Myth #2: If you lose your confidence, it's gone for good.* (No, you can always get it back.)

3. *Myth #3: Once you have confidence, you don't have to do anything to maintain it.* (No, you can unfortunately lose it at any time.)

Developing a confident mindset is like developing a healthy body. You don't build a great body overnight or by taking a magic pill. The "secret" to getting a great body is to develop positive habits that you repeat consistently over time. To build a great body, you have to consume the right diet and perform the right exercises. Similarly, a confident mindset is built through feeding your mind the right mental diet and by putting yourself through the right experiences.

**The first secret to career success is *Belief***
**(in yourself and in the importance of your work).**

## DON'T BE AFRAID TO FALL AT FIRST

Despite feeling as if my ankles might break in half when trying to balance on ice skates, I went ice skating several years ago with a girl I had been dating for a few months. Once we got started, it was evident that her ice skating prowess was far superior to mine, so I held her hand for support rather than hold the rail of the rink.

While I thought I could pass this off as a romantic gesture, it did not take long for her to comment on how hard I appeared to be concentrating. This was probably a polite way to ask me to stop cutting off circulation to her hand.

Several minutes later, I rested, while my date skated on her own for a few laps. As I hung out on the side of the rink, I talked briefly with a young boy who was taking a quick break as well. I joked about my struggles: "Hey buddy, this is not easy. I don't know how you do it."

The boy fired back: "It's easy! Wanna see?!"

"Sure, let me see what ya got," I replied, admiring his enthusiasm.

He then left the rail and proceeded to run (not skate) around the rink, moving at a speed 10 times as fast I had skated several minutes earlier, *with help*. While he did not fall during that lap, he fell plenty of other times throughout the night. However, rather than stopping or being embarrassed, he just kept getting back up, smiling, and trying to skate even faster.

As for me, I spent the night worrying about "looking stupid" by falling down.

The result? I "succeeded" in not falling, but I moved at the pace of a turtle, and I certainly didn't get any better at ice skating, even though I had *plenty* of room for improvement.

As you start any new job or career, remember that the only way to get better and be more successful is to fall down first.

> LEIBMAN LIFE LESSON:
>
> *Falling at first is not failing.*
>
> *Falling at first is the only way you can eventually succeed.*

## THE 10 COMMANDMENTS FOR CONCRETE CONFIDENCE

1. *Consume a healthy mental diet.* You can't build six-pack abs by eating cheeseburgers and French fries every day, and you can't build a confident mindset by filling your mind with content from trashy TV shows or materialistic magazines. Inputs produce outputs. Fill your mind daily with inspirational books, tapes, and CDs. You are what you eat, right?

2. *Talk to yourself the right way.* No, you are not crazy. All of us have a dialogue going on in our heads as well. So . . . what do you say when you talk to yourself? If you are like most people, you probably spend most of your day thinking about your flaws or what's wrong with your life. Most people say things to themselves that they would never dream of saying to anyone else. Start talking to yourself with the same respect you should show anyone else. Replace your negative self-talk with positive self-talk and watch your confidence go through the roof.

3. *Develop an attitude of gratitude and celebrate your life.* Being thankful for what you do have instead of bitter about what you don't have is one of the best ways to appreciate yourself and your life. Make a list of everything you have to be thankful for and everything you like about yourself (including your best traits and your proudest achievements). Then, review the list daily. This simple action has completely changed the way I view myself and my life.

4. *Never take a vacation from your values.* What happens in Vegas does not stay in Vegas; it travels back with you and stays in your memory. If you want to dye your hair blonde for a night or use a fake name at a club (I like to use "Rex" sometimes), that's fine. However, I know people who have done some really shady things on vacation that they would never dream of doing at home. When you throw your values out the window because you are away from home or because you think no one is watching, you forget to realize that *you* have to live with your decisions forever. Sacrificing your values, at work or outside of work, is one of the fastest ways to destroy your self-image. (If you have already taken a vacation from your values, forgive yourself for being human, and don't do it again.)

5. *Step out of your comfort zone every day.* Every time you step out of your comfort zone (no matter how small the effort), your confidence increases. Every time you allow fear to hold you back (no matter how small the effort), your confidence shrinks. Like a muscle, confidence can grow only when you challenge it, and it will shrivel up if you don't exercise it consistently.

6. *Surround yourself with winners.* Attitudes are contagious. If you consistently hang out with negative, defeated people, you will develop a more negative mindset. If you consistently hang out with happy, confident people, you will develop a more positive mindset.

7. *Take pride in your appearance.* Dress your best at all times, regardless of who you might see. You should dress your best for yourself. Stop making excuses, and get in the gym, too. It's hard to feel good about yourself if you don't like your body.

8. *Take pride in your environment.* If your hero showed up at your house tomorrow, would you be embarrassed to invite him inside? If so, you need to make some changes to your physical environment immediately. Why aren't you treating your environment with the same care that you would a stranger's? Clean up your home, workspace, car, and any other environment you spend time in. You deserve to be surrounded by cleanliness.

9. *Use comparisons carefully.* Don't use comparisons to other people to measure your self-worth (either to feel better about yourself or worse about yourself). Feeling sorry for yourself will not help you get where you want to be, and feeling better than other people will lead to arrogance and complacency. Only use comparisons to people you admire as proof/inspiration for what you can achieve in the future.

10. *Procrastinate on worrying.* Most worry is about potential events or circumstances in the future that probably won't happen anyway. Stay in the moment and just focus on *today*. In his best-selling book *How to Stop Worrying and Start Living*, Dale Carnegie refers to this as "living in day-tight compartments." *Planning* for the future is healthy; *worrying* about the future is not.

## BELIEVE OR LEAVE

No one was more passionate about working for the Washington Wizards than I was during my tenure with the organization. Sure, all of our employees thought it was "cool" to work for an NBA team, but no one had as strong an emotional connection to basketball as I did. Even though my playing career ended on a sour note, the game had brought me so much joy as a child and teenager, and I always felt a tremendous sense of pride as an employee for an NBA franchise.

I probably generated more new business for the Washington Wizards' sales department over a three-year period than anyone else in franchise history. All of the other people featured in this book have had tremendous success after landing their dream jobs as well. Are our achievements a coincidence?

No way!

The intense pride we felt for our work and our employers enabled us to reach levels of success we would not have reached in most other jobs.

Most people just plug along doing work they don't care about. Then, they feel bitter about their careers, and they inaccurately assume they were not blessed with gifts that high-achievers were born with. Here's a secret that most people don't realize: Anyone can be a high-achiever in the right job.

> LEIBMAN LIFE LESSON:
> *You can't reach your full potential unless you have your dream job.*

Every job (even dream jobs) will have ups and downs. Passion for your work is what will keep you going when most people want to whine or quit. Passion will take you to levels you would otherwise never be able to access.

If you ever find yourself working for an organization that you don't believe in wholeheartedly, then go back to the introduction of this book and start all over again.

*Believe or leave.*

I'm not saying you should quit your job any time you disagree with a policy or have a dispute with a colleague. However, there is no reason to pursue or maintain long-term employment with an organization you aren't extremely proud to be affiliated with.

## *Julie Willoz Got Her Dream Job with Disney*

I knew I wanted to work for Disney when I completed my first internship at the Walt Disney World Resort. Once I started to work full-time, my managers' dedication made a positive impact on me. While I worked full-time as an entertainment performer, I decided my ultimate dream job would be as a guest services manager.

At the time, I was only 21 and expected that I would need to work in a variety of other roles before being considered for that position. This did not deter me! I started speaking with all of my managers about my goal and requested advice to make myself the best cast member I could be.

The leadership was gracious to provide me with information and insight, leaving me inspired to put my best foot forward every day. One day I approached yet another manager for some mentoring advice, and he was impressed with my tenacity and proactive approach to growth. He told me that business operations was seeking vibrant new leadership, and I should apply. He also gave me the name of one of his contacts whom I should call for information about the job. Since I had not met any manager as young as I was, this all seemed like a long shot, but I went for it anyway. Looking back, I believe it was my professional and eager demeanor that got me an interview.

I prepared myself for the interview by reviewing all of my mentoring notes and common interview questions. During the interview, I showcased my knowledge of business operations, my passion for positive cast experiences, and my leadership style. A few weeks later, I was offered my dream job, becoming one of the youngest managers in the entire Walt Disney World Resort.

I got my dream job and so can you!

—Julie Willoz

# CHAPTER 9

# EXCELLENCE

### (SUCCESS SECRET #2)

> "If you are going to achieve excellence in big things, you develop the habit in little matters."
>
> —COLIN POWELL, FOUR-STAR GENERAL AND
> FORMER U.S. SECRETARY OF STATE

June 15, 2008: at Camp Moremi in Botswana

I thought it would be cool to travel as far away from Washington, D.C., as humanly possible. After resigning from my position with the Washington Wizards in May 2008, I negotiated a period of six weeks off before starting my job with my next employer. During this "mini-retirement," I decided to fulfill a *personal* dream (those are important, too) to travel to Africa to do a safari.

My solo adventure began with a 14-hour plane ride from Washington, D.C., to Johannesburg, South Africa. Then, I took two more flights, a long bus ride, and a short boat ride as I traveled through Zambia en route to Botswana. Finally, I reached the destination I had been most excited about when planning the trip. The site was Camp Moremi at Moremi Game Reserve in Botswana, a wildlife sanctuary considered to be one of the most beautiful regions in Africa.

By far, it was the most remote location I had ever been to in my entire life. I was thousands of miles from home and in the middle of the jungle. In addition, the camp I was staying at accommodated only 10 to 20 guests at a time.

While on safari, I saw lions, leopards, elephants, wildebeests, impala, crocodiles, hippos, warthogs, zebra, impalas, and all sorts of birds. However, I saw something even more amazing during my trip.

I was enjoying lunch outside on my last day at Camp Moremi when a boat pulled up to the shore right next to camp. The following night's guests had arrived. A group of nine people got off the boat and started to make their way toward me.

I could not believe my eyes.

One of the people in the group was a girl who played in my coed softball league back in Washington. Her family had booked a safari adventure at Camp Moremi for the week after my stay!

What does this have to do with your career?

If you think you can get away with something at work because your boss is not standing right next to you or because your boss left early for the day, you are absolutely out of your mind. Never do anything that would make you feel uncomfortable if people at work knew about it. Despite traveling halfway across the world (to one of the most remote locations on the planet), I *still* ran into someone I knew.

> **LEIBMAN LIFE LESSON:**
> *Assume you are being watched at all times, and assume that people you know are always around.*
> *It really is a small world. . . .*

## WHAT IS EXCELLENCE?

Excellence can be displayed in many ways. Here are some of them.

- ► Excellence is when you always do what you say you will, and a little bit extra.

► Excellence is when you do the right thing, no matter how it will impact you in the short term.

► Excellence is when you do the right thing, even when you think no one is watching.

► Excellence is when you take pride in your appearance, even when you think no one will see you.

► Excellence is when you never make excuses, complain, or feel that you are "above" any task.

► Excellence is when you never need to be asked more than once.

► Excellence is when you treat every person with respect, regardless of whom the person is.

> **LEIBMAN LIFE LESSON:**
> *Excellence is rare. It never goes unnoticed, and it is always eventually rewarded.*

► Excellence is when you make every person or project around you better.

► Excellence is when you pursue mastery and always strive to be your best.

► Excellence is when you can admit you are wrong and learn from your mistakes.

**The second secret to career success is**
***Excellence.***

When you are a person of excellence, word travels fast, and you become indispensable in your organization and industry. Your reputation will travel with you throughout your career, so make sure you develop a reputation worth having.

# WARNING: LITTLE THINGS MATTER

Upon learning about his next task, one of my former interns with the Wizards said, "Are you serious? You better get me season tickets for doing this one."

I simply responded by saying, "James, you just don't get it."

The following week, after receiving complaints from a number of employees (not from me), our vice president fired him.

At the start of your career or when starting any new job, be prepared to do some work that you may feel is beneath you. Do not look at these projects as insulting to your ability. Instead, view them as opportunities to prove your discipline, work ethic, and willingness to pay your dues.

I hate to break it to you, but when you start any job, you have to understand that your employer owes you absolutely nothing. After you get hired, no one will care where you went to college, no one will care what your GPA was, and no one will care about your past accolades or awards.

You will be starting from scratch, and you will need to prove yourself. Don't walk in with a sense of entitlement. Don't expect to have anything handed to you. Understand that every task is a test. You fail the test if you whine or complain or if you do a poor job. You pass the test and move on to the next (bigger and better) test when you do a great job and keep a smile on your face. You have to be a soldier before you can be a commander.

Excellence is not just about doing the right things. It's also about *not* doing the wrong things, no matter how minor they may seem to you. Here are 10 more things you should never do at work.

## 1. Never Arrive Late, and Never Leave Early

Leave yourself enough time so that you can arrive 15 minutes early for work every day and so that you can arrive five minutes early for every meeting. Always stay at least a few minutes after the workday ends as well. Projects have an eerie way of being assigned late in the day, and your boss will be irate if he can't find you because you ducked out early. I once had a boss who actually threatened to fire employees who showed up one minute late for work or who left one minute early. While that was extreme, every boss takes it as a personal insult when his employees cut corners. Don't take advantage of your organization by stretching your lunch hour either.

## 2. Never Treat Your Desk Like a Dorm Room

Dressing for success is not just about your attire: It extends to your office area as well. Walk into any CEO's office and look at her desk, and you will almost always find a workspace that is neat, organized, and free of clutter. There are a lot of factors that go into getting to the C-Level. Among them are being professional at all times and being well-organized and highly productive. Unfortunately, many young employees, especially those just out of college, treat their workspaces like dorm rooms. What impression do you think you are giving your colleagues and your boss if it looks like a tornado attacked your desk?

I once had an employee whose workspace looked like a garbage dump. His cubicle was full of trash, leftover food, and unorganized stacks of papers and folders. Not surprisingly, his performance was less than stellar. It's hard to be efficient if it takes you 15 minutes to find your stapler.

Another of my former colleagues actually had a life-sized Britney Spears poster in his cubicle. (This was back when Britney was hot.) Pictures of friends/family are fine. Posters of scantily clad celebrities are not.

By keeping your workspace neat and professional, you will appear to have everything under control (even if you really don't), and you will also be more productive and relaxed because you will have taken the time to assign a place for all of your stuff.

## 3. Never Be Too Casual on Casual Days

Casual Friday is the time to let loose and show off your style to the office, right? Wrong. I have seen colleagues wear tank tops, graphic

T-shirts, basketball jerseys, and cut-off jean shorts to work. I also once saw a woman wear a cut-off shirt and low-cut jeans, a combination that made her belly-button ring, lower back tattoo, and red thong quite visible. Just because you might be going to a club later that night does not mean you should dress for the club during the workday. Unless you work in the fashion industry, work is not the place to make fashion statements.

You shouldn't be wearing a three-piece suit on casual Fridays, but remember that you are still at work. Err on the side of being slightly overdressed at all times. Casual Fridays are also not excuses to come in with sloppy stubble or smelling like you were out doing tequila shots until 4 a.m. the night before. Your colleagues (especially senior management) will notice how you present yourself at all times. You can "let yourself go" on the weekends if you want, but always keep it professional during the week. People don't take slobs seriously.

## 4. Never Have Bad Breath or Body Odor

One of my prior employers sent out memos to the entire company on two separate occasions to report that HR had received multiple complaints about hygiene issues among the staff. Do you want to know the scariest part about this? Right after the first memo was sent, one of the biggest culprits came running over to my workspace. Hysterically laughing, he said, "Pete, can you believe that people aren't showering before work? I wonder who management is talking about!" I chose not to break the bad news to him. The second time the memo was sent, it was sent by a manager who was notorious for having bad breath. The staff got a big kick out of that.

It sounds extremely obvious to say that you should maintain great hygiene at work, but this is worth mentioning since there is always at least one person in every office (sometimes *several* people, unfortunately) with a body odor and/or bad breath problem. Do yourself and your colleagues a favor and shower before work each day, brush your teeth well, wear deodorant, and go light on any perfumes or colognes. You should also keep some gum, mouthwash, and a toothbrush in your desk drawer at work so that you can fumigate your mouth after lunch every day.

## 5. Never Stink Up the Kitchen

I can still remember the smell of a preservative-laden, Kung Pao chicken TV dinner that one of my colleagues used to enjoy for lunch. After she microwaved her meal, the entire office stank for hours. I have no idea how she actually ate that food, but the bigger issue was that people resented the fact that we had to smell the remnants all afternoon. Don't bring food to work that has an offensive odor. If your food spills in the refrigerator or microwave, clean it up. If you use china or silverware, don't leave it in the sink. It's also not acceptable to brush your teeth in the office's kitchen sink (yes, I've seen people do that). Treat any shared spaces at work with respect.

## 6. Never Get Drunk at Office Functions

Your company splurged for an open bar for the holiday party. Time to let loose and go nuts, right? Wrong. Everyone might enjoy hanging out with the office clown after work, but the office clown rarely gets promoted. Several years ago, one of my brother's colleagues got totally trashed at the office holiday party. From then on, he was known by senior management as "Sloppy Steve." Never let your guard down at work, even if someone in senior management is getting sauced. The senior vice president might be able to get away with having a few too many drinks—a new employee cannot.

## 7. Never Send or Store Anything Questionable on Your Computer

Several years ago, one of my colleagues was checking out a nude slide show of a famous supermodel on his computer. Midway through the slides, his manager walked up behind him to ask a question. If you think it's embarrassing for your parents to find you looking at nude pictures, imagine how it feels when your boss catches you viewing them at 11 a.m. on a Tuesday morning.

## 8. Never Create Unnecessary Noise

I once had an intern who forgot to take his cell phone with him when he went to lunch. For the next hour, we had to listen to a series of vulgar *South Park* ring tones whenever he got a text message or a call. Keep your cell phone on vibrate or silent at work. If you want to listen to music, do it at a reasonable volume. Just make sure your boss and colleagues are OK with you listening to music, and never let the music distract you from doing your job. Also, if you talk on the phone at work, speak at a low level. If you find something funny, control yourself. I had another colleague who used to laugh so loudly and uncontrollably that you could hear him across the entire floor of our office space. He was fun to go to lunch with, but it was embarrassing to speak to customers when he was experiencing one of his outbursts.

## 9. Never Botch an Email

While employed at a previous job, I received an email one afternoon from one of my colleagues. The subject line was "New account," and the email said the following:

> Hey Pete, I noticed you just inherited the account for Bill Jenkins. [Note: This was not his real name.] I just wanted to let you know what a jerk he is. He is very dishonest, always telling me that I promised him things I never did. You really have to be careful around this guy. Let me know if you have any questions.

After reading this message, I noticed that someone else had been cc'ed on the email by mistake. Guess who. . . .

Sending an email for something administrative (like "John, I received your fax") is a smart use of time. However, email should *never* be used for something that could be misconstrued or for something controversial or negative. You should also proofread and make sure no one is accidentally cc'ed on the message before you hit "send."

## 10. Never Talk About Your Employer Online

Just because you have gotten hired does not mean you are free to post whatever you want on the Internet. In May 2010, the Washington Wizards won the NBA Draft Lottery, earning them the #1 pick in the 2010 draft. One of my former co-workers (who still worked for the team at that time) got eager and posted a message on a Facebook group page for University of Kentucky alumni. He posted one sentence predicting that the Wizards would pick Kentucky guard John Wall with the first pick, and that alumni should contact him to get a great deal on tickets. Less than three hours later, his Facebook post was a headline on ESPN.com! As a result of his online comment, he nearly got fired.

> LEIBMAN LIFE LESSON:
> *Little things can be a big deal.*

### Laura Saldivar *Got Her Dream Job with* Teach For America

I graduated from college with a personal mission—I would use my life to make this world a better place, to bring a voice to those who so frequently go unheard, and to help others realize their fullest potential. I was attracted to Teach For America because the organization was committed to creating a movement to eliminate educational inequity in our nation's public schools.

I started off with an entry-level job at Teach For America's New York City headquarters. At that time, the organization was embarking on a five-year strategic plan through 2010 to grow its impact across the country. The plan included expansion into new regions, innovative initiatives for coaching teachers to produce significant academic gains with students, and a focus on positioning Teach For America alumni for leadership in a variety of sectors. Somehow, the sheer existence of this ambitious plan made my initial tasks feel more purposeful, more important, and more inspiring.

I decided that I would set a *personal* five-year strategic plan for how I wanted to grow my own impact by 2010. In five years, I vowed that I would lead the expansion of Teach For America in Texas. It was an ambitious plan, and I wasn't entirely sure it was feasible, but it motivated me to exceed the highest expectation in all aspects of my work. Five years after I moved to New York City and made my personal strategic plan, I was named the founding executive director of Teach For America–San Antonio, one of the organization's largest expansion regions in its entire history. In 2010, nearly 100 corps members were placed in the San Antonio Independent School District—the same school district I had attended as a student 10 years prior.

Our work, in partnership with the larger community, will ensure that one day, all students in San Antonio receive an excellent education. This mission fuels my fire every day.

I got my dream job and so can you!

—Laura Saldivar

CHAPTER 10

# PERFORMANCE

## (SUCCESS SECRET #3)

> "When we do more than we are paid to do, eventually we
> will be paid more for what we do."
>
> —ZIG ZIGLAR, AUTHOR OF *SEE YOU AT THE TOP*

June 19, 2003: at the Washington Wizards' offices (in my
cubicle)

I felt a cantaloupe-sized knot form in my stomach.

My workspace was in earshot of seven colleagues who would
hear every word I was about to say while making my first cold call
for the Wizards. All sorts of "what if" worries swirled through my
head. *"What if I say something stupid?" "What if I don't know
what to say?" "What if the person on the other end of the line hangs
up on me?"*

I dialed the number, desperately hoping that the person I was
calling would not pick up, allowing me to leave a message instead.
Unfortunately, I was met with "Hello?"

The next two minutes were a blur, but I managed to speak. The
prospect was polite but said she was "not interested." I thought to
myself, *"This is* not *going to be easy."*

Fast-forward three years to the day to June 19, 2006. That
morning, I was seated at my desk when the director of inside sales

came over and asked me to teach a new colleague how to make a cold call. As I made the call, I felt completely different from how I did three years earlier. There was no knot in my stomach, and I actually wanted the prospect to pick up the phone. Despite having hardly any sales experience, I had become the #1 salesperson for the Wizards (out of a staff of 25 much more experienced employees) in less than three years.

One of the "secrets" to my success was that I read (and applied) everything I could find on the subjects of sales, marketing, communication, and relationship building. I also called sales leaders from every other team in the NBA to brainstorm ideas on how we could each improve our performance. Had I just tried to figure out everything on my own, there is no way I would have gotten the same results as quickly.

The fastest, most efficient way to deliver results and advance your career is to find people who have already done what you want to do and study how they did it. Yes, it is that simple!

Why try to figure out how to do something on your own when you could learn from someone else who has already done what you want to do? You are reading this book, so I know I am preaching to the choir, but this is worth emphasizing. In just a few hours (and for an average cost of $10 to $20), you can learn what it took another person years to figure out. For example, this book is the culmination of 10 years of my personal and professional experience.

Unfortunately, most people never read a quality book after graduating from college. Then, they wonder why they are not achieving their personal and professional goals as quickly as they would like.

Do you want to be a leader? The first step is to become a reader. Then, take what you learn and apply it to your life and career. Make sure your education never ends after college. The world's most successful people have one thing in common: They are all voracious students.

If you think you don't have time to invest in self-education, you are missing the point. By investing time in self-education, you will save yourself time in the end because you'll suc-

> LEIBMAN LIFE LESSON:
> *Learn from the best, and you will surpass the rest.*

ceed faster. Even if you just invest 30 minutes each day during your commute (to read or listen to an educational tape), you will give yourself more than 100 hours of added education a year. Think of what an edge that will give you over your competition.

**The third secret to career success is *Performance*.**

You were hired for one reason: to deliver results. When you start any job, make sure you are very clear on what is expected of you, how your performance (and your employer's performance) will be measured, and where you are trying to get to next. In other words, you need to ask yourself the following questions:

► *How is performance being measured for my department/ employer?*

► *How is my performance being measured in my current position?*

► *What is the next level I want to reach?* (Note: The next level does not need to be an actual promotion.)

► *What is the #1 skill I need to develop to reach the next level?*

► *What is the #1 knowledge base I need to expand to reach the next level?*

Most people approach their careers backward, thinking that they'll add more value once they get promoted. It rarely works that way. You have to add more value first.


## TIME IS *NOT* MONEY

Everyone is "really busy." Get over it! Here are five secrets for maximizing your time so you can deliver results faster at work.

## 1. Follow the 80–20 Principle

The 80–20 principle states that 20 percent of your activities will yield 80 percent of your results. In other words, certain activities always provide more value than others. Spend the bulk of your time on whatever is most important for success in your job. Most people do the opposite. They waste all their time on minutiae, and then they think they are "too busy" to do what's actually most important.

## 2. Be a Machine

Create a system for everything you do at work so that you can be as efficient as possible. Always ask yourself: *"How can I/we do this faster, without sacrificing quality?"*

## 3. Focus

Multitasking is not when you perform multiple tasks at the same exact time. Multitasking is when you have *multiple projects in motion* at the same time. There is a big difference. Some people think they are being productive because they can function with 17 different windows open on their computer screen at once. All I can say in response to that is that there is no way you would be *less* productive if you focused on one project at a time. Interrupting yourself every two minutes (e.g., to reply to an email or send a text or post a new tweet) is the fastest way to destroy your productivity.

## 4. Reflect Often

Most people take the time to get organized and focused only at the start of a new year or right before going on vacation. Don't make that mistake. At the end of each week, invest one to two hours in cleaning up your workspace and inbox, reviewing the prior week, and asking yourself the following questions:

► *What were my biggest wins over the last week?*

► *What were my biggest challenges over the last week?*

► *What should I do next week to get where I want to be in the future?*

You should also invest 15 minutes to do this at the end of each workday. Set three to five main goals in advance of each week and set three to five mini-goals in advance of each day. Daily progress leads to momentum, and momentum leads to greater confidence and greater performance over the long term. Small actions (or inactions) add up quickly.

## 5. Take Control of Your Inbox

Do you get too much email? Well, join the club. Here are five easy ways you can regain control of your inbox so that you can be more productive at work:

1. *Pick up the phone.* If you find yourself spending more than five minutes writing an email, that's a sign you should be making a phone call instead. Email should be used mainly for administrative matters, not for anything complicated or open to interpretation. The exception is when you want to have written documentation for your communication.

2. *Save templates.* Create a folder in your email system for "email templates" or "common emails," and save copies of any emails that you send frequently. Then, rather than having to rewrite the same email 100 times, you can simply copy and paste the template and update whatever changes are necessary. Just make sure you personalize each email template before sending.

3. *Create email folders and use them.* Create folders for different categories of messages. For example, you could classify emails

by client, by project, and so on. Rather than keeping all emails in your inbox, this makes it much more manageable to find emails, and it keeps your inbox tidy. I also have an email folder titled "read later." Whenever I receive an e-newsletter or a message from one of my LinkedIn groups, I move it to my "read later" folder, which I check only on Fridays or weekends.

4. *Use the "delete" button.* Save the last message in an email thread and delete all prior emails. Clean out your inbox weekly and delete any messages not worth saving. More than 90 percent of all emails fall into this category.

5. *Keep email closed most of the day.* Do not keep your email system open all day. I used to do this, and I'd drop whatever I was doing every time an email popped up. My clients and colleagues loved the fact that I often replied in less than two minutes, but my work would constantly get interrupted. Even worse, if/when people did not hear back from me within 15 minutes, they would call to see why I had not responded yet. I had conditioned everyone around me to expect rapid responses. Keep your email closed most of the day, and check it every hour or a few times each day.

> **LEIBMAN LIFE LESSON:**
> *Time is more valuable than money. Once it's gone, you can never get it back. Invest it wisely.*

## BIGGER AND BETTER

"Mark, I don't think I can do this," I said to my boss, while looking up at the crowd of 1,500 people that had gathered at the Verizon Center for the 2005 Washington Wizards' Sports Careers Day. Up until that point of my life, I had never spoken in front of more than 15 people at a time. Now, I was just moments away from speaking to a group that was *100 times* as large.

"Pete, just grab a drink," Mark replied. "You'll be fine."

I went to the bathroom real fast and gathered myself. Then, I grabbed a drink (of water) before making my way back to the Verizon Center floor.

I nearly passed out in front of 1,500 people that day, but I survived and ultimately realized that I really enjoy speaking in public to large groups.

The Washington Wizards' Sports Careers Day was an annual event I created at the end of my first season working in the NBA. Through this program, students from the mid-Atlantic region would come to the Verizon Center in Washington, D.C., to learn about careers in sports. Several other NBA teams had similar events, and my boss suggested I look into creating one for our franchise. While nearly everyone else in the department had much more experience than me at the time, I believe my boss entrusted me with the project because of the way I had approached my smaller assignments earlier in the season.

Over my five-year career in the NBA, we used a variety of innovative marketing strategies to grow this annual event into the largest and most profitable program in franchise history. More than 4,500 students attended the December 2007 event alone. This project increased my confidence exponentially, while enhancing my visibility and reputation throughout the organization and the NBA. The event also eventually helped me get a book deal and launch a business and a nationwide speaking tour.

I hope it's clear that I'm not talking about my background to brag or impress you. I'm saying all of this to emphasize that your career is what *you* make it. Do great work, and great projects will find you. Then, it's up to you to maximize them.

*If you want to make more money and advance your career, you have to provide more value.* Period. Many people walk around whining about how their employer hasn't promoted them or given them a raise, yet they are doing nothing to increase the value they provide to their employer. You are not entitled to a raise each year simply because you showed up at work. You deserve a raise only if you helped your organization improve somehow.

Find creative ways to make your organization better, and you will be an extremely valuable, well-compensated employee. You will also have plenty of opportunities to move to other organizations if you still feel that your current employer isn't paying you what you are worth. Despite what many people think, creativity is a skill that can be developed. Here are five ways that you can be more creative so that you can deliver bigger and better results.

1. *Think outside of your box (i.e., cubicle).* It's hard to think outside the box when you are inside a cubicle that is the size of a box! Want to be more creative? Go outside. Even better, find a scenic, expansive place to do some thinking. Many of my best ideas have come to me when I've been driving, or outside at a lake, in the mountains, at the beach, and so on.

> LEIBMAN LIFE LESSON:
> *If you want to advance your career, you have to provide more value. Good things come to those who innovate.*

2. *Get away and explore.* Time away from a project will leave you refreshed when you come back to it. You will often be able to look at the project from a different viewpoint. I've had some of my best ideas while traveling, exercising, or trying out some kind of new experience. (Luckily, there is no video footage of my "new experience" as a student in a hip-hop dance class.)

3. *Ask the right questions.* When you ask the right questions, you get the right answers. Instead of thinking to yourself, *"Why am I not more creative?"* or *"How come I never come up with any great ideas?"* ask yourself empowering questions that get your mind headed in the right direction. Here are seven great questions you can ask yourself to unleash your creativity and your earning potential:
   · *How can we do this faster?*
   · *How can we make this bigger?*
   · *How can we make this better?*
   · *How can we make this more profitable?*

- *What can we do to retain more of our supporters?*
- *What can we do to increase support from our existing supporters?*
- *What can we do to attract new supporters?*

4. *Brainstorm with others.* You will never reach your creative potential alone. There is tremendous value in brainstorming with other people in your department/organization/industry and with people from totally different backgrounds. An outside perspective can often provide a fresh source of ideas.

5. *Read and study.* Read and study about your industry (and about success, in general), and watch your creativity skyrocket. Just start with 15 to 30 minutes of self-education each day.

# CHAPTER 11

# RELATIONSHIPS

## (SUCCESS SECRET #4)

> "Call it a clan, call it a network, call it a tribe, call it a family:
> Whatever you call it, whoever you are, you need one."
>
> — JANE HOWARD, ENGLISH NOVELIST

July 15, 2003: at the Washington Wizards' offices (in the board-room)

The entire sales department was on edge. An afternoon staff meeting had been called by the team president, Susan O'Malley. The plan was for Susan to meet with the sales staff to discuss several new policies and for the department to brainstorm business development strategies for the upcoming year.

I was less than one month into my tenure with the Wizards, and I walked to the meeting that day with one of my colleagues, another entry-level employee whom I will call "Ron." We sat next to each other when the meeting began, with a total of 30 people seated around a large table.

At the meeting, Susan told the staff about a new commission policy that was likely going to reduce the earning potential for most of the employees during the upcoming season. Ron raised his hand and said, "Susan, I do not understand the philosophy of this organization. Why does this company always look for ways to nickel-and-dime us?"

There was complete silence in the room, as 29 heads turned to Susan to see her response. As a 5'2" woman running an NBA franchise, she certainly hadn't gotten to the top by taking crap from entry-level employees. However, being the pro that she was, she remained calm, actually thanked Ron for his concern, and explained the policy one more time. Ron wasn't even worth her breaking a sweat, and we moved on to another topic.

I was blown away that Ron had had the audacity to question the president of the company in front of the entire staff. I was also impressed by the grace Susan demonstrated in her response. However, I learned a bigger lesson that afternoon when one of the older sales reps, Kevin, asked if he could talk to me for a minute.

> **LEIBMAN LIFE LESSON:**
> *You will be judged by the company you keep at your company. Hang out with the winners and avoid the losers at all costs.*

"Pete, what did you think of Ron's question in the meeting?" he asked.

"I couldn't believe he had the nerve to say something like that to the president," I responded.

"You're right," Kevin said, "but did you realize that you showed up for the meeting with Ron, you sat next to Ron in the meeting, and you also left the meeting with Ron? Susan doesn't really know you yet, so you have to be more careful about whom senior management sees you with. Ron's career is going nowhere. If I were you, I'd keep my distance from him."

I nodded my head, thanked Kevin for his valuable advice, and never made a similar mistake again.

Fair or unfair, judgments will be made about you based on the company you keep at work. Be especially careful as a new employee. You might not be able to avoid certain people altogether, but when going to meetings, office parties, and other staff functions, you can always control whom you show up with and sit with.

**The fourth secret to career success**
**is *Relationships*.**

Promotions are not based on just performance. Promotions are also based on office politics and your ability to connect with colleagues, subordinates, supervisors, customers, and other people outside your organization.

## THE SECOND MOST IMPORTANT RELATIONSHIP FOR YOUR CAREER

In Chapter 8, I discussed why the most important relationship for your career (and your life) is the relationship you have with yourself. The second most important relationship for your career is the relationship you have with your boss. No matter what you think of the person you report to, he or she will have a significant impact on the quality of your career now and in the future. Here are seven secrets for building a rock-solid relationship with your supervisor.

### 1. Make Life Easier for Your Boss

Send occasional progress updates, ideas, or good news to your boss to keep him in the loop. Volunteer whenever your boss needs extra help, and always do more than expected. Always ask your boss what you can do to improve yourself and your organization. If you are ever without something to work on, ask what else you can do. You should also never create unnecessary work for your boss. In addition, never display a poor attitude; you are only hurting yourself if you are difficult.

### 2. Make Your Boss Look Good to Her Boss

Unless you report directly to the owner of your organization, your boss will have a boss also. Ask yourself, *"How is my boss's performance being measured, and what can I do to make her look good to her boss?"* Your subsequent actions will not go unnoticed. In addition, if someone ever asks you about your boss, always remain positive, even if you think your boss is a moron. It does you no good to badmouth the person who has more influence over your career than anyone else. If your boss is an idiot, the person above her surely knows it already anyway.

### 3. Never Go Above Your Boss

There is no faster way to violate trust. The only exception is if your supervisor is doing something illegal or very alarming.

### 4. Propose Solutions When You Encounter Problems

You should always handle problems (with projects, colleagues, or customers) on your own as much as possible. If that's not feasible, always be prepared to offer some potential solutions, rather than expecting your boss to solve your problems.

### 5. Ask Questions Intelligently

As a new employee, you will likely have lots of questions. Rather than harassing your boss every 15 minutes, keep track of your questions, and ask them at one time as much as possible. Also, make sure you never ask the same question twice.

### 6. Accept Your Manager's Pet Peeves or Weaknesses

One of my former managers had a huge pet peeve for lateness and for using the Internet for personal matters. Rather than accepting his policies on these issues, many employees in the department whined publicly and privately. The result? My boss dug his heels in and actually started suspending people when they violated his "rules." One of my colleagues actually lost all Internet/email privileges on his computer for a six-week period, forcing him to use the intern station whenever he wanted to use the Internet! Every boss has some pet peeves, and no boss is perfect. Deal with it.

## 7. Choose Your Words Carefully

It takes only a few words to make your boss hate you. Make sure you never utter these words to your supervisor:

- *"Sorry, I've been busy."* (Everyone is busy. Being busy is never an acceptable excuse at work.)

- *"I'll try my best."* (Your boss doesn't want you to "try your best." Your boss wants you to get it done.)

- *"That's not part of my job."* (If your boss asks you to do something, it's part of your job.)

- *"Why do I have to do this?"* (Do you want to know why? Because your boss said so.)

- *"Sorry, I forgot."* (You are not allowed to "forget" at work, unless you want your employer to "forget" to keep paying you.)

- *"I didn't know that's what you wanted."* (Your boss does not expect you to be able to read her mind, so she expects you to ask if you are not sure.)

## DEALING WITH DIFFICULT PEOPLE IS EASY

"Pete, whatever you do, stay away from John at all costs," she warned. "The guy is miserable."

This was the advice given to me by a colleague on my first day at one of my former jobs, and when I met John for the first time, it was pretty clear how he had developed his reputation. Not only was he unfriendly—he was actually rude. He *never* smiled, and everything about his body language and communication was a total turnoff. As a result, I, along with everyone else in the company, kept my interactions with him as brief and infrequent as possible.

Several months into my new job, I was in a meeting with several of my colleagues, including John. We were pitching a partnership proposal to a group from a local organization. John had played a large role in what we were presenting, and the person leading the project noted his contribution in front of everyone: "John was the brains behind this project."

The leader from the organization we were meeting with loved John's ideas as well. He responded by adding: "John, this is absolutely brilliant. This is the best idea that has been presented to our organization in a while."

I will always remember what I saw next.

It looked as if John went through instantaneous plastic surgery. Several wrinkles in his face seemed to evaporate, the usual redness in his cheeks seemed to disappear, and he flashed a smile (the first one I had ever seen from him) that could have gotten him a modeling gig with Colgate toothpaste.

This guy was not a bad person. He just needed some genuine appreciation! He had gotten caught up in a vicious cycle of poor confidence leading to a poor attitude leading to poor relationships with other people leading to even poorer confidence. No matter where you work or what you do, you will have to deal with difficult people. Here are seven secrets for handling them with ease.

1. *Don't take it personally.* In 2009, I was involved in a networking group. One of the women in the group was incredibly abrasive and critical. I later learned that her young daughter had just been diagnosed with cancer. That tragedy did not give her the right to disrespect us, but it made it easier for me to understand why she did. At work, you usually won't know what's going on in everyone's personal life. If someone is difficult, it probably has absolutely nothing to do with you, so don't take it personally.

2. *Consider your role.* Having said that, you might have had something to do with the other person's poor attitude! As hard as it might be, when someone is critical, you have to listen to *what* is being said and ignore *how* it is being said. Did you do something that brought on the reaction? For example, one of my former roommates once lashed out at me when I mistakenly threw out some of his kitchen tools during an overenthusiastic New Year's Day cleaning session. While I did not like *how* he discussed this with me, *what* he was saying was totally accurate. I was 100 percent wrong throwing out several of his items without asking if he still wanted them. Ultimately, I was the cause of his reaction, and I took accountability by agreeing to replace the items.

3. *Fight fire with water.* If someone lashes out at you, it's very tempting to fire back. However, that will only make the situation worse. Always keep your cool and stay calm, no matter how hard that might be. If necessary, excuse yourself for a few minutes and get some fresh air. Let the other person vent, and choose your words very carefully when you respond. You will be amazed at how people calm down when you hear them out and consider their perspective.

4. *Kill them with kindness.* You should never let people walk all over you just for the sake of keeping the peace. However, recognize that difficult people usually just have low self-esteem and are actually crying out for some genuine appreciation. Especially if the person is a subordinate or colleague, consider being a source of encouragement.

5. *Talk it out in person.* Never go behind someone's back because that will only make her even angrier if it gets back to her. I made that mistake once at the start of my career when I tried to get a manager to resolve a dispute I had with a colleague over an account. When she learned that I had questioned her to my manager, she went nuts. You should also not rely on email or texting to discuss disputes. Talk face-to-face (ideal) or via phone if an in-person meeting is not possible. Discuss-

ing a conflict over lunch can also serve to clear the air and help you repair or improve a strained relationship.

6. *Involve other people carefully.* If you have failed to settle a dispute, then (and only then) consider bringing in other people to help. Just be certain that the difficult person knows you will be bringing in someone else.

7. *If all else fails, minimize interactions.* Sometimes, no matter what you do, you will not be able to improve your relationship with a colleague, boss, or customer. In that case, either eliminate all interaction with the person (I know that's not possible if the difficult person is your boss!) or minimize the time spent with him as much as possible. Your #1 responsibility is to keep yourself happy. Not everyone at work will like you, especially if you are a young, ambitious employee willing to do dirty work that other employees are not. It's nice to be liked, but it's better to be respected. Do great work and carry yourself the right way, and "haters" will always *respect* you even if they don't *like* you out of jealousy.

> LEIBMAN LIFE LESSON:
> *No one is born with a rotten attitude. People lash out when they have low self-esteem or when they don't know how to deal with stress and adversity in a healthy way.*

## NEVER STOP NETWORKING

Remember that life is a team sport, and networking is a *lifelong process* of building friendships. Here are 10 rules for building rock-solid professional relationships in and out of your organization.

1. *Strengthen your foundation first.* The better you get along with yourself, the easier it will be to form relationships with others. You also will not be given the opportunity to lead oth-

ers (as a supervisor or project manager) until you have first proven that you can lead yourself.

2. *Be positive.* No one at work (or anywhere else) wants to hear your complaints. If you consistently whine about what's wrong in your life, people will avoid you like you have a deadly disease. I used to work with a guy who had a different ailment, injury, or problem for every single day of the month. He was not a bad person, but people really disliked him because of how depressing he was to be around.

3. *Be reliable.* There is no faster way to violate trust and damage a relationship than to be unreliable. While most people will brush this off as common sense, very few people *always* do what they say they will.

4. *Always be completely honest.* I remember a time when one of my former bosses called a staff meeting to tell us about a new policy. He tried to tell us that it would somehow be better for our salary structure, even though it was quite clear that most of the staff would be negatively affected by the change. After work that day, I went out for beers with a few colleagues, and everyone agreed that we would have been able to deal with the news if our boss had just been honest with us. We all resented the fact that he thought he could fool us. People are going to figure stuff out anyway, so you might as well be transparent.

5. *Say thank you often.* Success is always a team effort. If you ever win an award or have an opportunity to be recognized in public, make sure you also recognize the people who helped you get there. Either way, always thank the people behind the scenes as well.

6. *Give your undivided attention.* One of my former bosses always used to reply to emails while attempting to talk to people in his office. The entire staff found it disrespectful, and

he probably could have saved time if he had focused on one task at a time anyway (either his emails or his in-person conversations).

7. *Remember birthdays.* One of my former employers used to send monthly emails to the staff to let us know when everyone's birthday was. I used to write everyone's birthday in my Outlook calendar, so that I could email people a short birthday message on their special day. One of my colleagues once called me from home (he had taken off for the day) to let me know how much my gesture had meant to him. No matter what people say, they always like to be acknowledged on their special day. Thanks to Facebook, you can even get reminders of people's birthdays.

8. *Make people look good to their bosses.* If someone does a great job, let her boss know. It will make its way back to her, and it will make you look good to her boss, too.

9. *Say congratulations and mean it.* Whenever someone gets promoted at work or does an outstanding job on a project, the entire organization or department usually receives a message about it. Always be one of the people who helps the person celebrate his achievement. You want people to celebrate when you succeed, don't you? Pass along praise as well. If someone mentions something positive about one of your colleagues, let your colleague know about it. Again, this makes everyone involved look good.

> LEIBMAN LIFE LESSON:
> *Rock-solid relationships can make your career recession-proof. Never stop networking.*

10. *Ask for and value people's opinions.* This is one of the reasons why I admired Susan O'Malley, the former team president of the Washington Wizards. She was always interested in my opinion, even though she was much more experienced.

Because she made me feel important, I would have run through a brick wall for her. You don't have to crack the whip as a boss or project manager when your employees feel appreciated and invested in their work.

## *Josiah Beam Got His Dream Job with Southwest Airlines*

During my junior year at Northwood University, a strong business-oriented university in Dallas, Texas, I made up a list of the top five companies I wanted to work for. While studying to complete my bachelor's degree in marketing, I completed many case studies on Southwest Airlines and its unique business model. It was because of these case studies and Southwest's success stories that I knew that it was my top choice for employment.

I had a family friend who worked for Southwest Airlines, so I reached out to her for help in applying for the internship program. She wrote a recommendation letter for me, and I was called in to interview for a position. Unfortunately, I was turned down after my first interview.

Although I was upset, I followed up with my friend to let her know that I was not selected. This follow-up communication afforded me one more chance to interview for a different internship within the company. A few hours after that interview, I received "the call" notifying me that I had been selected as a Southwest Airlines intern!

I interned with Southwest Airlines for one year, and during that time, my mentor showed me how to grow my network within the company. Following my internship, I gained full-time employment and have been promoted twice in less than three years.

As for my advice, you must know that networking is one of your strongest tools for getting hired and advancing your career. Employers hire people with character, and if a proven individual vouches for you, your character has been confirmed for the time being. Keep in mind that a recommendation comes with responsibility. You are not only representing yourself but the person who recommended you. Once you land that internship or first job, remember that you are now interviewing for your next position. Networking can help you get there.

I got my dream job and so can you!

—MICHAEL "JOSIAH" BEAM

# CHAPTER 12

# OUT-OF-OFFICE LIFE

## (SUCCESS SECRET #5)

"Nobody on his deathbed ever said, 'I wish I had spent more time at the office.'"

—PAUL TSONGAS, FORMER U.S. SENATOR

7:12 p.m., Friday, November 17, 2007: at the Verizon Center (in my private office)

I cleaned off my desk, turned off my computer, and locked the door to my office. Once again, I had chosen to stay late after work, even though there was no real reason to do so. There was nothing urgent or very important that needed to be finished, and my boss didn't even know I would be there that late.

As I started to make my way downstairs to the trains located underneath the arena, I noticed that I was the only person entering the station. I approached the turnstiles for the Metro and reached into my pocket to grab my train ticket. Then, I looked up.

All of a sudden, 200 fellow 20-somethings appeared from around the corner, headed in the opposite direction. They had all just arrived at the Verizon Center. I remembered there was a Dane Cook show at the arena that night.

The contrast of how they and I would be spending the next few hours was striking to me. The only activities I had planned for the weekend were to watch the Wizards' road game at my house that night and to work the Wizards' home game the following evening. My peers were headed to a comedy show with their friends, while I was headed home to hang out with my leather recliner and 50-inch plasma TV.

That night served as a microcosm for my life during my first five years after college. My career was priority #1, and everything else was an afterthought.

As a result of the distorted way I viewed my life in my early 20s, my attitude was completely based on what was going on at any given time at work. When things were good at work, I felt like I was on top of the world. When the NBA was in the off-season or things were bad at work (even a dream job has occasional downs), I would feel terrible. I had no perspective of the larger picture, and the result was that my confidence and happiness were on a constant roller coaster even though I loved my job.

**The fifth secret to career success is your**
***Out-of-Office Life.***

Most career books miss this altogether or barely address it. Most employers do not care what you do in your free time (as long as you don't do anything to embarrass them). However, you need to understand that your life outside the office has a huge impact on your life inside the office. Being proactive with your out-of-office life will make you happier and improve your performance at work. I often wonder how much better my experience could have been with my dream job in the NBA if I knew then what I know now about taking charge of the other areas of my life.

## TAKE CHARGE OF YOUR OUT-OF-OFFICE LIFE

Make sure you are headed where you want to be in *every* area of your life, not just your career. If not, determine what you need to change to get there, and create a plan for making it happen. Instead of just setting New Year's resolutions, look at your goals in monthly increments to make them more manageable. Most important, spend one to two hours every weekend (all year long) reflecting on the previous week, planning the following week, and thinking about the overall direction of your life and your contribution to the world. I could have enjoyed my 20s a lot more (and achieved even more at work) if I had started this practice as a student.

If you don't think this weekly ritual is worth doing, what are you doing in your free time that is more important? Most people unfortunately spend more time worrying about the lives of their favorite celebrities or athletes than they do planning their own lives. As you get older, your values will also change. Mine certainly have.

If you don't stop along the way to make sure you are headed in the right direction, you can end up far away from where you really want to be. Here are six points you should keep in mind about your life outside of work.

## 1. You Only Live Once

If you love your job and never have anything to look forward to outside work, you will never leave the office. You'll end up working late on Friday nights. You may even go to the office on the weekends, which I also did on a number of occasions when I worked in the NBA. This lifestyle can eventually catch up with you. You can burn yourself out, and you can even start to resent your job, even though your job is not the real issue. Professional achievement can provide only so much happiness and satisfaction.

Start by focusing on your favorites. Make a list of your 10 favorite things to do outside work, and make sure you do all of them as often as possible. Then, make sure you get away occasionally. The best time to take a break is when you think you don't have time for a break! Travel and explore your area (and the world) as much as you can. While I have definitely splurged for some exotic vacations over the last few years, travel need not be expensive. Some of my favorite excursions have been local day trips or road trips on my own or with friends.

Last, broaden your horizons. Try a food you have never eaten before, take a class on a subject you know nothing about, read a book you would normally not pick up, check out a new museum, take a new route to work, or do something purely recreational that you have never considered before or that you have always wanted to do. Over the last three years, I've flown a helicopter (with help), taken a class on hip-hop dancing (I secretly wish I could move like Usher), eaten wildebeest (it tasted as bad as it sounds), and fired a semiautomatic rifle (don't worry, no animals or humans were harmed).

## 2. You Get Only One Body

Do you want to live longer, look better, feel better, and make more money? Then take care of the only body you will ever have. You can't treat a Ferrari like a pickup truck and expect it to drive like a Ferrari. Your body is more valuable than a Ferrari, so take care of it! A healthier, stronger body will give you the confidence and energy needed to do things most people would consider "impossible." It's also a good long-term strategy.

Did you know that most cancer cases are linked to diet and lifestyle? Did you know that being overweight increases your chances of developing dementia, Alzheimer's disease, and other mental disorders as you age? Did you know that eating right and exercising more often can improve your sexual functioning? (Whenever I am tempted to be unhealthy or slack off from the gym, I remind myself of this one.)

As a certified personal trainer and nutrition coach, I am going to give you six fitness/nutrition secrets for increasing your energy and performance at work (and for building a six-pack that would make "The Situation" from *Jersey Shore* jealous).

1. *Control your mind.* Like any change, it all starts with your "why." You have to find exciting reasons why you want to change your body. Without this motivation, you are just relying on willpower. Be careful of your associations as well. Food should be viewed as a source of energy most of the time and

as an *occasional* source of pleasure; most people look at eating backward. In addition, exercise need not be boring (I don't enjoy running on treadmills either). Work out with your friends or get involved in local sports leagues or group exercise programs at a gym.

2. *Eat a great breakfast every day.* Breakfast is the foundation for how you will feel and what you will eat and be tempted to eat for the rest of the day. Stick to lean proteins (e.g., egg whites, skim milk, soy milk, nonfat or low-fat yogurt and cottage cheese) and good carbohydrates, such as fresh fruit, 100 percent whole-wheat bread, bran cereals, or oatmeal. You can also just mix up a smoothie or protein shake with skim/soy milk and some fresh fruit or yogurt. Ditch the egg yolks, donuts, bagels, muffins, pastries, pancakes, waffles, and sugary coffee drinks.

3. *Eat fresh, not processed.* Perhaps the main cause of obesity is overconsumption of processed carbohydrates. Your body was not built to eat many of the foods created in the last 50 years. Focus on high-fiber, fresh foods like beans, vegetables, fruits, and whole grains. Minimize your consumption of processed foods from boxes or cans.

4. *Save your calories for foods.* You are what you eat *and* what you drink. If you drink a glass of orange juice at breakfast, a can of soda at lunch, and a sweetened iced tea at dinner, you will consume one pound of sugar each week! Think of the damage that does to your mind and body. Calories from alcohol (sorry) can be deadliest of all. Stick to water, skim milk or 1-percent milk, and unsweetened tea as much as you can.

5. *Don't take nutrition advice from marketers.* In fact, be skeptical of foods that advertise just how "healthy" they are. Always read nutrition labels, and make sure you know what you are putting in your body. For example, did you know that *ground turkey* has 20 times as much fat as *ground turkey breast*? The only reason I know this is because I read food labels.

6. *Do cardio* and *strength training.* Cardiovascular training will make your heart stronger and help you burn calories. However, strength training provides benefits not attainable through cardio alone, such as improvement in lean muscle mass (which speeds up your metabolism naturally) and strengthening muscles and bones (which makes you less likely to get injured, especially as you age).

## 3. The Greatest Present You Can Give Someone Is Your Presence

I really struggled with the transition from high school to college, especially on the basketball court. My parents were a real source of strength that year. During my freshman season, my father made it to nearly every basketball game I had, despite the fact that he lived more than 200 miles from my college, and despite the fact that I didn't always play that much. For one game in particular, he got out of work early and drove five hours to watch me play at Gettysburg College. Then, he drove five hours back home, went to bed at 2 a.m., and got to work on time the next day. (I could share similar stories for my mom as well.) I do not remember what my parents got me for my 10th birthday, for my 16th birthday, for my 21st birthday, or for any other birthday. However, I will *always* remember my dad driving nearly 10 hours in one day just to watch me play 15 minutes in a game. My point here? Never put your career ahead of the people who matter most to you.

## 4. There Are Other People Like You Out There

Every Monday night from 7 to 8 p.m., I torture 75 fellow 20-somethings, and they love me for it. Well, most of them do. I run a sports conditioning class at my local health club (think high school sports drills, but with Jay-Z blasting in the background). By teaching this weekly class and creating a group on Facebook for members of the class, I made more than 100 new friends in less than a year. Outside of class, we do happy hours, barbecues, house parties, beach trips, group runs/races, and more intense events (go to toughmudder. com for an example). No matter what is going on in my life, I always look forward to spending Monday nights with 75 peers who share my passion for fitness.

No matter what you love to do in your free time, there are like-minded people out there who are just as passionate about your hobbies as you are. Find those people. I really could have used this personal peer group earlier in my 20s. Meetup.com is a great website to find events and groups for any location, hobby, or interest. If you don't find a group there for you, start one.

## 5. You Can't Marry Your Career

A dream job is not a soul mate. After college, you learn very quickly that your dating life can dry up fast if you don't make it a priority. I asked Pai Dayan, founder of VIP Date Coach, to share some tips for taking charge of your dating life. Here is what he had to say:

► *Get clear on what you want first.* Are you looking for a long-term relationship, or do you want something more casual?

► *Look your best.* Others will take notice, and your confidence level is sure to climb. You deserve to look and feel your best. Go shopping and treat yourself to some new clothes. Do not try to be someone you're not, but amplify and accentuate your positives.

► *Build a support system.* Surround yourself with people who are dating and who have positive feelings about love and relationships. You need people who will be there with you during the inevitable ups and downs of dating.

► *Get out of the house.* Sign up for and attend as many club, society, sports, networking, and charity events as you can. The possibility of meeting a like-minded person to date is far greater in person than when sitting at home watching TV or surfing the Net.

➤ *Enjoy the process.* Enjoy dating for what it is. It is nothing more than the process of meeting new people and socializing with individuals who may or may not play a bigger role in your life down the road. Most people you meet have something interesting to offer. Keep an open mind.

Got a dating question? Visit Pai's website at www.vipdate coach.com or email him directly at vipdatecoach@live.com.

## 6. The Best Way to Feel Better About Yourself Is to Think About Yourself Less

Rick Warren wrote in *The Purpose Driven Life* that "Humility is not thinking less of yourself; it is thinking of yourself less." I could have used Warren's wisdom when I started my career after college. While I was a customer-service superstar and I treated everyone I met with respect, I rarely went *out of my way* to serve people who were not connected to my career. By focusing completely on myself, I frequently lost perspective of how fortunate I was, and I also ended up making career decisions based on money.

> LEIBMAN LIFE LESSON:
> *Your career cannot fulfill all of your needs as a human being. Take charge of your life.*

Find a cause to support in your free time outside work, even if you donate only a few hours each month. Over the last few years, I've mentored high school students, coached youth basketball teams, played bingo with the elderly, and volunteered at dog shelters. Every time I stop thinking about myself and start thinking about others, I end up feeling better about myself. No one has ever had a quarter-life crisis because he spent too much time serving others! Give back every chance you get.

Since I could not possibly cover everything in this chapter about creating your ideal life as a young professional, here are four great books that can give you more support:

1. *Naked! How to Find the Perfect Partner by Revealing Your True Self* by David Wygant

2. *I Will Teach You to Be Rich* by Ramit Sethi

3. *The 4-Hour Body: An Uncommon Guide to Rapid Fat-Loss, Incredible Sex, and Becoming Superhuman* by Timothy Ferriss

4. *Conquering Your Quarterlife Crisis: Advice from Twentysomethings Who Have Been There and Survived* by Alexandra Robbins

CHAPTER 13

# BE AN
# ENTREPRENEUR

"We need to stop looking at work as simply a means of
earning a living and start realizing it is one of the elemental
ingredients of making a life."

—LUCI SWINDOLL, AUTHOR OF *DOING LIFE DIFFERENTLY*

9:03 p.m., March 5, 2008: at the Verizon Center (on the event
level of the arena)

We were getting killed. As the fourth quarter began at the Verizon
Center that night, the Orlando Magic were beating the Wizards by
22 points. With the game all but decided, I took the elevator from
the event level up to my private office on the fourth floor of the
arena and closed my door.

Over the last few years, I had developed a tremendous passion
for personal and professional development, and I took out the book
I was studying at the time: *Maximum Achievement* by Brian Tracy.
As I read the book that night, one of the questions in the book
stood out to me: *"What would you do if you knew you would not
fail?"*

The answer came to me right away: *"I would start my own
business."* It was something I had dreamed of doing ever since running my first lemonade stand as a little kid.

However, my mind immediately responded to my answer by providing a variety of reasons for *not* starting a business: *"You don't know what type of business to start. . . . You don't have any idea how to get started. . . . You don't have anyone to help you. . . . Starting a business is probably really expensive. . . . Starting a business is really risky. . . . You might fail. . . ."*

Having already talked myself out of the idea, I ignored my answer and just kept reading. Even though my job in the NBA had been a dream job for five years, I had reached a point where I was ready for a new challenge. I felt like I had achieved my dream of becoming a successful executive in an NBA front office. Rather than continue down my path toward senior management with the Wizards or with another NBA team, I was ready to start a new dream. However, I had no idea what to do next.

Less than two months later, one of my VIP clients made me a great offer to head up a business development unit for his company. The company really wanted me, and the owner had a very successful, entrepreneurial philosophy, so I accepted the job, excited about the income potential and the new challenge.

### 7:56 p.m., Tuesday, June 2, 2009: Arlington, Virginia (in the bedroom of my home)

All I could think to myself was, *"What just happened? This was not how I planned it to go down."*

Just 15 months earlier, I had felt like I was on top of the world at work. I had my dream job in the NBA, my own private office inside the Verizon Center, access to all sorts of perks, respect throughout my company and industry, and an army full of satisfied customers, partners, and colleagues.

Now, as I sat in my bedroom, I felt stuck in a new career that I saw no future in, in a job that was a very poor fit for me. It was clearly time for another career change, but after an arduous process of self-reflection, career assessments, and discussions with career counselors, I was still lost.

Feeling defeated, I glanced at the bookshelf in my room, where I had stacked more than 100 books I had read in my free time over the last few years on all sorts of topics related to personal and professional development. Three thoughts immediately entered my mind.

First, I thought to myself how much I loved reading and studying those books. Then, I thought to myself how cool it would be to have the same impact on other people that those authors had made on my life. Then, I asked myself, *"Why not?"*

> LEIBMAN LIFE LESSON:
> *There is no risk in going after your dreams. The only risk is in not going after your dreams.*

Unlike the year before, when I had talked myself out of the idea of starting my own business, I realized now that burying a dream was a recipe for disaster. One month later, I resigned my job to pursue my next dream job as an entrepreneur, speaker, published author, and career coach. While it has not been an easy journey, it was one of the best decisions of my life.

## THE ADVICE IN THIS BOOK ALSO HELPED ME GET MY SECOND DREAM JOB

The process of getting my second dream job—starting a successful business and landing a book deal with a great publisher—was eerily similar to the process of getting my first dream job working for an NBA franchise.

Initially, I just took a leap of faith, even though I had no idea where to begin and no step-by-step blueprint to follow. My enthusiasm was then met with a barrage of doubters who questioned my decision and tried to temper my enthusiasm for a variety of reasons. Like the first time I went after my dream job, I was initially disappointed by this reaction. However, once again, I then got angry and more motivated, as I decided that I would prove people wrong and use their doubts to fuel my fire further.

Like the first time I went after my dream job, my initial faith ultimately morphed into a burning conviction that I would succeed. To be clear, this is not to say that my fears and internal doubts were eliminated. Not at all. However, I decided that I would not let fear and worry prevent me from achieving something I truly believed was my destiny. Unlike my basketball career, I decided that I would keep going, *even though* I felt fear.

In case you are wondering how I got my book deal, I'll give you one guess. (After you guess, keep reading to see if you are right.) This time, however—in contrast to when I got my job with the Wizards—it was a little more of an accident, since I somehow didn't learn my lesson from getting my dream job the first time. It is amazing what you can achieve when you actually take your own advice!

On April 10, 2010, I attended a networking event for the Washington, D.C., chapter of the National Speakers Association. During a break, I spoke briefly with a fellow member of the group, Anne Loehr. Anne is an expert on generational differences, so I was intrigued by her work, and we had connected several months earlier. She mentioned to me that day that she was working on a career book for young professionals. I told her that I was writing a book on that very topic, a project I had started the year before, even though I did not have an agent or publisher yet.

The following month, Anne introduced me to her agent, who wanted to represent me and help me sell my idea to a publisher. (Anne and I initially planned to write a different book together, and I appreciate her letting me run with my own project.) Eight months later, my most recent dream became a reality when my agent helped me get a contract from AMACOM (a division of American Management Association) to write this book.

Still have doubts that networking works? Well, it helped me get my dream job twice while I was in my 20s.

## DO YOU WANT TO BE AN ENTREPRENEUR?

If you have any interest in starting your own business, let me give you some quick advice. First, remember that *every business starts as nothing more than a dream*. Over the last few years, I've attended public and private seminars run by a variety of multimillionaire entrepreneurs. Regardless of the event or the speaker, each person spoke about his willingness to start at the bottom and build slowly. Each person also spoke about overcoming tremendous obstacles along the way.

It's easy when you start a business to look at how far you have to go or to look at businesses that are bigger than yours. Use your comparisons wisely. Every successful entrepreneur was once just someone with a dream who was willing to take the plunge. Why can't you do the same?

My second point is this: Be clear on whether you want your venture to be a hobby, a business, or a nonprofit organization. It can be only one of those things. This is especially important to remember if you start a service business. I initially felt guilty about charging for my services because I did not start my businesses for the money. I quickly learned that I would have to go back to eating ramen noodles if I gave away everything for free! I also realized that people started taking me more seriously when I increased my prices. If you charge too little, people will assume you are selling crap, even if you are selling gold.

While you might not have ever thought of running your own business, I'd encourage you to consider it. You don't need a lot of money saved up to start a small business, as an Internet or service business can be started for less than $1,000. You also don't need to quit your full-time job to become a full-time entrepreneur. Many people run part-time businesses in as little as three to five hours per week or seasonal businesses that operate only during the summers or certain other times of the year.

If you are thinking about starting your own business, you better be all or most of the following:

► *Passionate.* Being an entrepreneur is not easy, so you better have a very strong "why" for starting a business. Passion is an entrepreneur's fuel. Passion makes you resilient and keeps you going when inevitable challenges arise.

► *Confident.* As I have mentioned throughout this book, if you don't believe in yourself, no one else will either. This becomes even more important when you are running your own company.

► *Focused.* Your business will fail if you try to be everything to everyone. Make sure you know what you are selling (and not selling) and whom your customers are (and whom they are not). Be careful not to try to do too many projects at one time either. An idea or project is worthless if you don't take the time to execute it from start to finish.

► *Competitive.* Running a business is a competition that never ends. There are no "off days" when you start your own business. You better be prepared to bring your "A" game every day.

► *Disciplined.* The *best* part of running your own business is not having a boss. The *worst* part of running your own business is not having a boss. Without someone looking over your shoulder, it is easy to get off track, so you better be very self-motivated.

► *Results-oriented.* Like everything else in the "real world," entrepreneurial success is all about results. Deliver great work and exceed expectations for your partners and customers, or be prepared to be replaced by someone who will.

## GET HELP

Since there is no way that one short chapter could give you all the tools needed to start your own business, I thought it would be smarter to direct you to some of the best resources for entrepreneurs that I am aware of. Here are three groups and websites you can check out:

1. Score.org (SCORE is an organization that provides free business counseling)

2. LinkedIn.com (you can join worldwide groups for entrepreneurs through LinkedIn)

3. Meetup.com (you can find events in your area for entrepreneurs through Meetup)

Here are my five favorite books on entrepreneurial success:

1. *The Millionaire Messenger: Make a Difference and a Fortune Sharing Your Advice* by Brendon Burchard

2. *Awakening the Entrepreneur Within: How Ordinary People Can Create Extraordinary Companies* by Michael Gerber

3. *What No One Ever Tells You About Starting Your Own Business* by Jan Norman

4. *The McGraw-Hill Guide to Starting Your Own Business* by Stephen C. Harper

5. *The Small Business Owner's Manual* by Joe Kennedy

## Andrew Horn Got His Dream Job by Being an Entrepreneur

The most important step you can take toward finding your dream job is figuring out what you truly care about. I can recall three specific conversations I had growing up that helped me do just that.

The first took place at a dinner table in Charleston, South Carolina. The question posed to me was a simple one: "What are you passionate about?" My friend Stever added, "Don't think of your passions as events or trades. Think about them as values and virtues."

He helped me realize that sports and photography were just mediums that helped me pursue and engage my real passions, things like competition, fitness, and creativity. When you think of your passions in this way, it's much easier to identify jobs that will help you utilize them. After I did that, I quickly realized I needed to figure out what I was really passionate about.

Another turning point came for me after I read the book and saw the movie *Into the Wild* and decided that if I was going to "find myself," the open road would be a good place to do it. So I drove to Alaska with my dad. My biggest breakthrough on our journey happened while driving through Michigan. My dad asked me what was the last thing that I had done that I was proud of. It led me back to my time working in Chicago as the first-ever intern for an organization called Dreams For Kids. I realized that having pride in your work is usually a sure sign of passion and fulfillment, so you should seek to identify experiences that you were proud of.

Another day, one of my friends asked me a simple question: "What aren't you doing that you'd like to be?" I said simply, "Starting my own nonprofit." What happened next is the answer to how I got my dream job. I asked myself, *"What's the next thing I can do that would move me closer to that goal?"*

I called the founder of Dreams For Kids in Chicago, Tom Tuohy, and told him I wanted to bring Dreams For Kids to D.C. He said, "Go for it."

That night, I Googled "how to start a nonprofit in D.C." and filed the necessary applications. Four months later, a piece of paper came in the mail informing me that Dreams For Kids was legally approved to operate in D.C. We were off and running.

I got my dream job and so can you!

—ANDREW HORN

# CONCLUSION

**10:37 a.m., Tuesday, July 28, 2009:** Arlington, Virginia (in the kitchen of my home)

All I could think to myself was, *"Did I just make a huge mistake?"* Only 15 days earlier, I had officially left my position with my last employer to pursue my dream of starting my own business and landing a book deal. However, I had no clue how to begin my journey, and I was overwhelmed with fear, doubt, and uncertainty.

I had a free round-trip voucher for a trip on Southwest Airlines to anywhere in the United States, so I decided to cash it in. I booked a morning flight for the following day, a Wednesday, from Washington, D.C., to Las Vegas and a return flight from Denver back to Washington for Friday night. My plan was to drive from Las Vegas to Denver by myself. I figured that two days alone on the road would help me clear my thoughts and regain my composure.

Upon landing in Las Vegas, I got in a rental car and started my drive. I am probably the only 20-something male who has ever flown into Las Vegas and *immediately* left town to drive through the desert alone!

Over the next 46 hours, I drove nearly 1,100 miles by myself through some of the most barren terrain I had ever seen. I also crossed through four of Utah's national parks. Their beautiful, massive landscapes inspired me to keep thinking big. When I finally arrived back in Washington that Friday night, I felt refreshed and confident in my decision to go out on my own.

The day after returning from my trek, I went to a barbecue at a friend's house. Throughout the evening, a number of people asked me about my next career move. Most of these conversations were not very memorable. However, there was one exchange that I will always remember.

Upon learning about my decision to pursue my dream to start a business, one of the people in the group said, "Starting your own business, huh? That's cool. So. . . . How long you gonna give it?"

I hesitated for a moment, and the group looked at me, waiting for my response. It was an interesting question, and one that was probably innocent. Had he asked me that question five days earlier, I am not sure what my response would have been. However, two days on the road had helped me strengthen my commitment to my dream. I looked him right in the eye and said, "How long am I gonna give it? This is not an experiment. This is my dream. I'm gonna give it as long as it takes."

When I went after my first dream job to work for a pro sports franchise as an inexperienced, shy, 21-year-old student, there was not a day that went by when I did not have doubt or consider giving up. I cannot express in words how glad I am that I kept going. I often wonder how much less exciting and less meaningful my life would have been if I had followed the easy, traditional path and accepted some dull job instead.

When I started my dream of becoming a published author and successful entrepreneur, again, there was not a day that went by when I was free of doubt or fear. However, I always thought back to the question from that barbecue and to the commitment I made *to myself* with my answer.

I'd like to end this book by challenging you with the same question about your dream:

*"So. . . . How long you gonna give it?"*

You *know* there is only one right answer. *Go out and make it happen!*

• • •

P.S. When you succeed, I want to hear about it! You can reach me directly at www.PeteLeibman.com.

# APPENDIX A

*Leibman's Lexicon*

## THE NEW GLOSSARY FOR CAREER SUCCESS

**Advice Appointments:** 15- to 30-minute appointments (in person or on the phone) when you ask Game-Changers for advice on breaking into a certain field

**Affiliations:** organizations you are a member of through your personal life, your academic life, or your professional life

**Apply Aggressively:** when you go above and beyond the standard job application procedures to stand out in a good way

**Cold Networking:** the process of introducing yourself via phone or the Internet to Level 3 Contacts who are Game-Changers

**Compelling Cover Letter:** a Marketing Asset that brings your résumé to life

**Cool Networking:** the process of introducing yourself in person to Level 3 Contacts who are Game-Changers (this is what most people think of when they hear the word *networking*)

**Current Contact List:** a list of your personal, academic, and professional contacts in your current network

**Debrief:** a review process after a job interview when you reflect on the interview and plan your next steps

**Dream Job:** a job that combines your passions and talents in a way that is meaningful to you

**Dream Job Description:** a detailed summary of what you want from your career

**Elegant Elevator Pitch:** an introduction for yourself in a networking situation that is clear, compelling, and concise (five to 10 seconds max)

**Email/Voicemail Marketing Machine:** a Marketing Asset that impresses potential employers during communications

**Game-Changer:** a successful senior executive in your ideal industry with the power to hire you or the ability to influence other people with the power to hire you

**Google Alert:** an automatic notification you receive when a specific word or phrase is published online

**Hard Sell:** a direct approach in which you ask if an organization is hiring (much less effective than a Soft Sell, when you just ask for advice)

**Hidden Job Market:** jobs filled behind-the-scenes through personal contacts (most jobs are filled through this channel)

**Hitchhiker:** someone who asks other people to do part of his job search for him

**Informational Interview:** a 15- to 30-minute appointment with someone working in a field you are considering (not to be confused with an Advice Appointment)

**Insider Information:** information provided by a Game-Changer about best-practices for breaking into an industry (also includes information about trends or best-practices for a certain field)

**Job Board:** an online resource where jobs are advertised to the public (the majority of jobs are not filled through these channels)

**Job Search Networking:** the process of generating job leads, referrals, and information from other people

**Job Search Office:** a location where you conduct most of your job search activities

**Job Search Teammate:** an accountability partner who supports you during your job search

**Killer Close:** a 30- to 60-second statement at the end of an interview that discusses why you want a specific job and why you should be hired (similar to the Smart Start); can also be used to overcome any objections from a hiring person

**Lemonade Stand Principle:** a principle that states that older people like to help younger people who are ambitious and enthusiastic

**Level 1 Contacts:** people you already know, such as your friends, family, or professional contacts

**Level 2 Contacts:** people you do not know (yet), but who have something in common with you (also known as "hidden" contacts)

**Level 3 Contacts:** people you do not know (yet) who do not share any common connections or affiliations with you

**LinkedIn Group:** a group of LinkedIn members with a common interest or background

**Marketing Asset:** a self-marketing tool that increases your chances of getting hired

**Networking:** a very misunderstood term that is nothing more than a lifelong process of building friendships

**Pumped-Up LinkedIn Profile:** an online Marketing Asset that is better than a résumé on steroids (according to LinkedIn expert Lewis Howes)

**Recommendation Report:** a Marketing Asset featuring one- to two-sentence endorsements from your references

**Results-Oriented Résumé:** a Marketing Asset that focuses on how you have made other people or organizations better

**Risk Remover:** a relevant work sample and/or action plan that you bring to an interview to eliminate concerns an employer has about hiring you

**Rock-Solid References:** strategic endorsements that increase your chances of getting hired

**Smart Start:** a 30- to 60-second statement at the start of an interview that discusses why you want a specific job and why you should be hired; this should be your response when an interviewer says, "Tell me about yourself"

**Soft Sell:** a subtle approach in which you ask someone for advice (much more effective than a Hard Sell, when you start by asking for a job)

**Strategic Success Story:** a powerful sales strategy when you use a specific example to prove that you have a relevant trait or skill

**Success:** a term you have to define for yourself . . . .

**Target Market:** a list of your ideal employers (usually consists of 10 to 20 organizations)

**TV Channel:** a Marketing Asset you can set up at www.youtube.com to increase your chances of getting hired

**Warm Networking:** the process of connecting with your Level 1 Contacts, while also using your Level 1 Contacts and your affiliations to connect with your Level 2 Contacts

**Winner's Mindset:** confidence in yourself to keep going even when inevitable challenges arise

# APPENDIX B

*Leibman's Lists*

## THE TOP RESOURCES FOR AMBITIOUS
## YOUNG PROFESSIONALS

## TOP BLOGS

For more career success secrets, visit my website at www.PeteLeib man.com, where you can receive free email, video, blog, and social media updates from me. In addition, here are other leading career advice blogs (listed in alphabetical order by first name) run by experts that I respect and encourage you to follow as well:

1. http://blog.AlexandraLevit.com by Alexandra Levit

2. http://blog.brazencareerist.com by Brazen Careerist

3. http://www.CareerRocketeer.com by Chris Perry

4. http://www.personalbrandingblog.com by Dan Schawbel

5. http://www.EmilyBennington.com by Emily Bennington

6. http://HeatherHuhman.com by Heather Huhman

7. http://www.JibberJobber.com/blog by Jason Alba

8. http://www.JayBlock.com/category/jays-blog by Jay Block

9. http://www.lifeaftercollege.org by Jenny Blake

10. http://careerenlightenment.com by Joshua Waldman

11. http://www.careerrealism.com by J. T. O'Donnell

12. http://www.JullienGordon.com by Jullien Gordon

13. http://www.KeithFerrazzi.com by Keith Ferrazzi

14. http://www.LindseyPollak.com/blog by Lindsey Pollak

15. http://www.keppiecareers.com by Miriam Salpeter

16. http://www.mscareergirl.com by Nicole Crimaldi

17. http://blog.PenelopeTrunk.com by Penelope Trunk

18. http://cornonthejob.com by Rich DeMatteo

19. http://www.onedayonejob.com by Willy Franzen

## TOP BOOKS

The following 10.5 books have all had a huge impact on my life, and I strongly encourage you to study them as well:

1. *The 7 Habits of Highly Effective People* by Stephen R. Covey

2. *The Success Principles: How to Get from Where You Are to Where You Want to Be* by Jack Canfield

3. *What's Holding You Back?: 30 Days to Having the Courage and Confidence to Do What You Want, Meet Whom You Want, and Go Where You Want* by Sam Horn

4. *Never Eat Alone and Other Secrets to Success: One Relationship at a Time* by Keith Ferrazzi

5. *Living the 80/20 Way: Work Less, Worry Less, Succeed More, Enjoy More* by Richard Koch

6. *Unlimited Power: The New Science of Personal Achievement* by Anthony Robbins

7. *The Magic of Thinking Big* by David J. Schwartz

8. *Maximum Achievement: Strategies and Skills That Will Unlock Your Hidden Powers to Succeed* by Brian Tracy

9. *The Psychology of Winning* by Denis Waitley

10. *The Luck Factor: Changing Your Luck, Changing Your Life, the Four Essential Principles* by Richard Wiseman

10.5 *Success Magazine* published by Darren Hardy

# INDEX

# ABOUT THE AUTHOR

Pete Leibman is the founder of Dream Job Academy and the Creator of The Washington Wizards' Sports Careers Day, programs attended by thousands of people since 2004.

When he was only 21 years old, Pete landed his "dream job" working in the front office of the NBA's Washington Wizards. He went on to be their #1 Salesperson of the Year for three straight seasons and was promoted to management in under two years.

Pete founded Dream Job Academy to help job seekers achieve greater satisfaction and success in their careers. Pete shares his career advice with thousands of people each year, and he has been invited to speak at some of the world's best colleges, including Stanford University and Johns Hopkins University.

To receive a FREE career success video course from Pete, or to learn how you can bring Pete to speak to your group, visit www.PeteLeibman.com.